Undressing the Elephant

Why the spread of good practice isn't working in healthcare;
presenting symptoms and suggested treatment

Sarah W. Fraser

First published in 2007 by Sarah W. Fraser

Contents

Foreword

This is my impatient book. On 30th April 2006 I stood with thousands on the Mall in front of the US Capitol at a rally in support of those killed in genocide in Dafur, Sudan. By that date around 200,000 lost their lives and over 2 million people were displaced in refugee camps. However, as I stood there at what was a very peaceful and spiritual experience as multiple faiths came together to support those who could not speak for themselves, I had a shocking thought. **Each year, almost the same number of people die in the USA from hospital acquired infections and preventable medical errors**.

Yes, a 1999 Institute of Medicine (IOM) report suggested that 90,000 Americans died each year from hospital acquired infections (HAI's) and 98,000 from medical errors that are preventable. Statistics from the NHS in England are a little less easy to come by, though a figure of 3,000 deaths from medication errors has been quoted and numbers of people harmed by HAIs ranges from 5,000 to 12,000 and above. This comes to an estimated total of 180,000 deaths in the USA and around 15,000 deaths or injuries in England – from just these two preventable areas. This is not including patients who do not receive evidence based care; for example the USA National Committee of Quality Assurance suggested that a further 80,000 Americans die each year because they do not receive appropriate evidence based treatment for diabetes, heart disease and high blood pressure.

Let's make these figures more real. Assume an average large airplane, and the ones I am on these days seem quite full, is carrying around 250 passengers. This equates, for both the USA and UK figures on infections and safety, to nearly two jets crashing each day, every day, every week, every month, every year – no survivors. In the US there would be 11 crashes per week, and 2 in England.

And remember these are preventable deaths. And this is only the estimated calculation for hospital acquired infections and preventable medical errors. I have not included those who die because they do not receive care that is simple and known about.

For example, an aspirin, where appropriate, if you have had a heart attack, may save your life. This has been known about in the evidence for decades yet constant studies demonstrate too few patients receive the guidance and support to take it. This is a simple piece of good practice to improve morbidity and mortality.

What left me wondering on that sunny day in Washington was both the differences and similarities between what was happening in Darfur (and many other countries round the world), and this problem we face in healthcare in the US and England (and similar healthcare related issues in other countries around the world).

Without a doubt the conditions of those who undergo degrading, frightening, terrifying, life-threatening and life-destroying experiences in war torn countries can barely be imagined by those who have not endured them. Their suffering is at one end of a continuum.

At the other end are those in our "care"; and I put that word in parenthesis on purpose. The difference is perhaps in the intention. We set out to help, to make better, to "do no harm", yet end up providing an experience that for many, very many – turns out to do the opposite.

My issue is this. At what point does the intention move away from harmless ignorance? To one where, for example, by not applying known, simple knowledge that will prevent an error or improve the odds of survival (like washing hands may reduce the likelihood of increased infection rates), we become complicit in the consequence. This also brings into question much of the construction of western medicine, the high value placed on autonomy and the complex ethics underlying the pricing, supply and demand dynamics of the market models used by many health systems. These issues are outwith the specific remit of this book though their context will have a bearing in many circumstances.

Already one hospital in England has had a criminal case against it, and lost, in the circumstance of a patient dying after acquiring an infection whilst in their care. The consequences for the doctors involved, the care team and the management team was considerable. And of course, the consequence for the patient's family is without adequate description.

Five years ago I wrote and subsequently published two books on the topic of the spread of good practice. I have written academic papers and contributed articles to journals on various topics related to both theoretical concepts and practical aspects of the matter. My journey in the past seven years has led me through a doctorate on the subject and I have devoted much of my business practice to working on projects, large and small, designed to scale up good practice across systems and within organisations.

What have I learnt from all this?

That the concept of "spread" and the business of "spreading good practice" as we continue to apply it in healthcare, may be a large part of why "spread" doesn't happen. I include myself in part of this challenge and in the past 18 months have conducted my own theoretical and experiential research testing new models. I've also reflected on why good practice doesn't spread, and this book captures my work, hopefully in a form that you will find useful. I have intentionally avoided theory; you can get that elsewhere.

I am easily distracted and don't have the best of memories so I have over many years developed the habit of keeping all my notes in journals. These are motley collections of anything from telephone messages, notes from meetings, to insights, reflections, notes for books, notes from discussions with colleagues etc. In writing this book I have reviewed my notes to discover the patterns, to identify the common questions I kept asking myself and to see where the most common difficulties and stumbling blocks that most of my clients appeared to be encountering with their spread programs lie. In these notes were also my reflections and insights from readings outside the regular published literature and I have developed these insights to try to provide new direction for some of the sticky spread and adoption problems in healthcare – all in an attempt to break free from the old thinking.

This is an alternative view – and specifically so. Each of the chapters will identify the basic presenting symptoms then describe the condition. You will then be provided with some suggested treatments and ideas for preventing future occurrences. Finally there are some thoughts about the future outlook with further readings on the topic should you require it.

I have tried to use examples where I can and have made these as real life as possible. The approach, style and content of this book does not make it politic to use case studies from my own consulting practice or other published work, other than that which is public knowledge in the literature. As you read through these "conditions" I am sure you will have your own a-ha moments as you recognise some of the stories.

It's not my intention to teach the basics of "spread". If you wish those, please refer to my earlier book, "Accelerating the Spread of Good Practice; a Handbook for Healthcare Practitioners" and there is a second book for those who have completed their improvement project and are looking to push the solutions across an organisation or system – "Rolling out your Project; Thirty-Five Tools for Healthcare Improvers" go to www.sfassociates.biz for details and links to bookstores.

Oh, and this book is intentionally irreverent. So if you are easily upset, or are a slave to "the" or "a" theory, then look away now.

Me – I thought it was time to move on and that included putting aside much of what I have talked about, written about and taught. And yes, that means eating some sour humble pie. Funny thing life, the reality of doing projects, some reflective learning and wonderful relationships and conversations with colleagues in the past 18 months have led me (and I believe some of them) to so many new points of learning – that no amount of theoretical literature reviews and ivory tower work could have led us to.

My wish is you'll be able to take something from what's in here and add it to your own learning process, building on your own special knowledge and experience. Let's add to the new wisdom of what works and most of all, really make a difference where it matters.

Email me with your thoughts – whatever they are

contact@sfassociates.biz

and keep checking the website for fresh resources and free downloads

www.sfassociates.biz

Chapter 1

An awkward case of Pilotitis

- Successful changes have been completed by an enthusiastic individual or team

- Initial eager adoption rates suddenly hit the wall

- Someone wanted some results quickly

- You had a quick start to your project with some "Me First" participants and this meant you also had some very early results.

- You may not have known what was "best practice" to start with so you had to run some test sites to find this out

- Some people (you may call them resistors) start to complain that your solution (that you call good practice) won't work in their context, their team, their organisation, their backyard

- Great project results, characterised by repetitive Plan-Do-Study-Act cycles, that eventually, often after the project reporting ends, turn the solution into something else because they begin to resolve an entirely different problem - maybe for the right reason!

DESCRIPTION

This condition is pervasive as can be found in all healthcare organisations and systems attempting to make changes through project orientated methods. It is particularly found where money is provided, and where money can be used, both to fund the invention and production of new ideas as well as the improvement and general running of the healthcare system undertaking the work.

Pilotitis is frequently underdiagnosed mostly because it is not painful in its early stages. Often celebrated as an early success, quick fix projects may be rapid to appear. One of their symptoms is their inability to integrate with the rest of the organisation's aims and structure. It is in the later stages that pain sets in, when integration is difficult, when others find it difficult to adopt the perceived good practices and when initial enthusiasm and funding or project related initiatives for the pilot run out and end.

Pilotitis occurs when the "Me First" groups, or maybe they are asked to be "First" groups by their sponsors, create and run a project on something quite new and they are successful in achieving their goals.

Let's think about this. We can take any example, whether it be from a hospital, community care, a mental health team, a high street pharmacy or a primary care practice, where the theory and the practice works the same. In this instance I'll use an example that links to improving care for patients with chronic diseases and is one that is system wide though an important one for primary care – the use of registries.

So, if we have an organisation that pilots, with the use of some funding, how registries may be beneficial for improving care for patients with diabetes, because their details are on record, they can be identified and risk assessed etc, then some data can be developed as to their use. Let's assume this organisation has seventeen primary care practices who could potentially adopt this good idea.

The leadership of the organisation funds and tracks a pilot scheme with two practices, we'll call them the pilots. Both of these pilots are practices with good Information Technology (IT) systems and they have experience in improvement work. The leadership chose them because it was important for this project to be successful and credible in the eyes of their peers. They also wanted some quick results. They needed success. Also, the pilot sites wanted to be involved. They were motivated to participate.

So consider this. They are early adopters – they are ahead of the curve. The two pilot sites are by definition outside the norm. Yes, really. Draw a normal distribution curve yourself, right now. The pilot sites are out there on the left, in the margins of the curve.

The good news for the leadership is that because the pilot sites are outside the norm, they have joined in early and delivered results early. If the leadership intention is to deliver a one off quick delivery of results, then this is a good strategy. However, if the strategy is to spread the good practice across the organisation there is some bad news.

Pilotitis is one of the most severe conditions restricting the spread of good practice. Why? Consider this. The pilot sites that have developed their successful change, have come up with the following three significant differences.

Firstly their *context*, their environment is outside the norm; they are different from their peers, the other fifteen (or least ten or twelve) of the primary care practices. In this registries example the pilot practices will most likely have better IT systems to start with.

Secondly, the *culture* within the team carrying out the work will be different, with the majority of the individuals within it being early adopters and less risk averse than those in many of the other practices. They may also have more available and willing access to information, as well as more experience in the improvement change process.

Finally, and perhaps most importantly, the *solution* they will create, will be one that is specific to their context and culture and it will by definition be one that will look and feel like something that is outside the norm to anyone who is "inside the norm". This is absolutely critical when it comes to the spread of good practice.

Do you think it is reasonable to expect 70% of people, those "in the norm" to adopt a solution ("good practice") developed "outside the norm"? Now, this isn't just one of my kooky ideas. There is a lot of evidence behind this thought and we will return to this in future chapters. It is a concept that is well known about in industry and one that is worked on in product development and product implementation. What concerns me is that somehow in healthcare we have developed an arrogance that when we have found a cool idea we think that that one single idea, with a bit of reinvention at the edges, needs to be swiftly pushed through the system, and that will solve our problems. And when the method doesn't work we either blame the method, or mostly, which to me seems quite unfair, we blame the people who didn't do the work of adopting. Or we say "it can't be done".

I say, it can be done. Though it is hard work. It requires multiple flexible strategies with built in feedback systems. More fundamentally it may mean we have to redesign the good idea, the good practice – continually – and for each group of adopters and context. And it means we have to rearrange some of our mental models and keep learning.

SUGGESTED TREATMENT

This is one of those situations where the best option is to avoid the problem in the first place (see preventable action below), however, if you find yourself with this awkward condition then there are some strategies to help you recover. Each situation will be different and this chapter can't cover them all, so I also suggest you check whether what you are experiencing may also be covered in some of the other chapters as well.

The main point of resistance that you may experience is usually around the *solution*, the successful change. While you may perceive the problem to be the individual or teams "resisting" adopting the change, the block is most likely to be in the change itself. There is a whole chapter dedicated to this problem – it is called "Crossing the Canyon" – also fondly known as the Deep Depression. This is the symptom where we get spread occurring in up to a quarter (20% - 25%) of our target population and then it grinds to a halt, never going any further.

So if we have a solution that was perfect and worked well for a pilot group that is outside the norm, namely it had some special characteristics, we shouldn't be surprised that the change may need some redesign in order for it to be more acceptable to the individuals and teams who we are perceiving to be a little resistant to taking it on. A good start is to listen to their gripes and complaints. In them is a real story. Listen long enough and help them keep focused on the benefits of the change and between you a resolution will emerge. However, it will take time, and there will most likely be some renewed testing of the change and maybe even some bigger changes required for the solution – but then, you should be reaching a bigger target audience – your norm group.

Another technique may be to involve others, not from the pilot group, as early on in the process as possible. You can do this by holding focus groups, advisory committees, review teams, communication awareness sessions, steering groups, pairing up with an observer from outside the team, anything as long as you don't actually increase the actual project team size as that will slow down delivery of the improvement work itself. You're looking to increase awareness of the change initiative and at the same time involving others in the discussion process so they can have time to prepare and maybe even influence the development of the pilot solution so it does not turn into a heavily customised product. A by-product of involving others at this stage is facilitating a sense of ownership of solutions. Early participation in the process is a great enabler for the change process.

PREVENTING FUTURE OCCURRENCES

This is the one condition where prevention is better than cure so the emphasis in this chapter is on how to avoid getting into difficulty in the first place.

Start every project with the full knowledge that pilotitis is likely to occur. Leaders need to consider their strategy before choosing pilot sites and teams. If the results are to be spread, then this must be taken into account. Similarly, for those who put together a bid of work for funding for projects and the ultimate dissemination of their results, need to take this into account and to demonstrate how they will counter their possible case of pilotitis.

You may decide, in a specific instance, that you won't be needing to spread the results. If you do plan to encourage others to adopt any successful changes then think carefully before you start and plan accordingly.

- To what extent is the individual or team carrying out the change considered "outside" their norm? How many improvement projects and initiatives have they participated in previously? Is it time for new players to join the team?

- What special circumstances are at work for this team that may not be available for those who are most likely to have to adopt the successful changes? How can the impact of these be reduced?

- How can the pilot project team be made more permeable through the use of outside influence, checks and balances; especially through contact by those who might be viewed as potential "resistors"? (Note that the term "resistors" is a prejudice that may turn out to be unhelpful.) Reviewers like these may ensure solutions are developed that suit the "norm" population.

- How early can the results be made known so they can be shared when half formed? There is evidence to suggest that good ideas spread more easily than changes that have been set in stone. This is because they are more easily adaptable by others who have a chance to reinvent them to suit their own context.

- Maybe sometimes we need to be more patient and not go immediately with the "Me Firsts". Can you diagnose who might be more of an "in the norm" team and although they may take longer to agree to start the project and to deliver a result, know their solution may be more acceptable to others and thus may spread more easily.

- Be constantly aware of developing innovator labs; these are sites and teams who always test things out. Try to spread the budget and pilot project money about, regardless of how desperate you are for quick fix results.

PROGNOSIS

Pilotitis can cause what looks like a patchwork quilt of improvement initiatives throughout a system, with empty slots of potential adoption. The outlook, in general, is not good when you get an awkward case of pilotitis. Do your best to prevent it.

FURTHER READING

Baker, Sunny & Kim, The Complete Idiot's Guide to Project Management (2nd Ed), Alpha Books, 2000: Exactly what it says…

Fraser, Sarah W., Accelerating the Spread of Good Practice; A Workbook for Healthcare, Kingsham Press, 2002: This will give you an introduction to any of the spread and adoption concepts and theories covered in this book, as well as many other comprehensive and more traditional references.

Chapter 2

Low hanging fruit syndrome (a.k.a. picking the population of least impact...)

PRESENTING SYMPTOMS

- Successful changes are completed yet on average not much overall impact is achieved

- Project teams demonstrate improvement on their individual charts, yet there is a sense of disappointment by the sponsor that the overall goal wasn't met or the underlying target didn't really shift

- Initial round of projects got great results, and then when asked to do a second round on the same topic the results were disappointing, despite a lot of hard work by everyone

- Someone always seems to get good results on their improvement projects but you don't

- There are concerns about sustainability (proven or otherwise) of results

DESCRIPTION

Anita Roddick, social entrepreneur and business woman who used to own the Body Shop business is credited with saying, "If you've ever spent the night in a tent with a mosquito then you know that small things really do matter."

The **population of impact** is the small, *purposely and analytically identified*, target group where if you place your efforts for change, will have the greatest overall benefit.

I'm not a detail person and I'm definitely not a statistician and it was probably for this reason that it took me many years of working on improvement projects before I really understood what the population of impact really meant. It is not about broadly identifying the target group of people to work with. It is not even a little bit of analysis checking who might be the most interesting group to work with. It is definitely not the group who volunteers to work on the project, though that is often the most prevalent group both joining the project and often the group targeted to work on.

What I have learnt is that if we want to make an *impact*, and the key word here is impact, on improving outcomes for patients in healthcare, then we need to do an inordinate amount of diagnostic work upfront, before the action starts, to identify the population of impact.

There's nothing new in this. It is good old fashioned quality improvement work, though in the haste of many of the projects I have seen in action, this does tend to get forgotten.

Let's look at an example of what happens when we go off beam and then track back to the underlying behaviours. In a large primary care group practice they have identified that 500 of the total 1000 of their patients who have diabetes have reported in a survey that they are unhappy with the care they are receiving and these same patients also appear not to be receiving the type of care that current evidence suggests would be appropriate. So the leadership team asks the local quality improvement co-ordinator to run some projects in each of their 10 primary care practices to improve the diabetic care for these patients.

Each of the 10 practices enthusiastically sets out on implementing the best evidence into practice using a variety of techniques. In a matter of months they each can demonstrate that for a sample of their patients they have implemented a variety of new initiatives ranging from group visits, newsletters, in one they have implemented a new clinic, in another medication reviews and the like. They hold a review session where everyone shows a poster with charted improvement results. It is likely these very specific improvement results are focused narrowly on areas on which they have chosen to work, may only reflect a very specific clinical focus, few may show other outcomes (balancing measures) and in my experience very few report on unintended consequences generated in the system.

However, despite these reported successes, on a repeat patient survey 350 patients still reported dissatisfaction and the overall clinical results showed that many patients were still not receiving the test results and care they needed. So what is going on? Despite all this hard work and enthusiastic activity at the practice level, something is missing. Impact.

If, before starting the action phase of the project, the quality improvement co-ordinator, working with the primary care practices, had spent a few weeks, sometimes it is months, doing some detailed analysis understanding the target population - to find the population of impact, she may have identified the unique group to benefit *directly* from the proposed changes.

If you have the choice between working with 89 diabetic patients on whom you can make a 7% improvement, or 13 patients on whom you can make a 56% improvement, which group will you decide to work with? In some primary care practises they will identify that a small number of patients account for the majority of their poor results. If they work to improve the care for these few identified patients they may make a large impact on the overall. This is often the case with medication spend. Rushing to test a group visit model with a few patients for whom there are little or small issues reported may help you test out a new way of working, however, it may have little impact on those patients who require solutions to their problems.

Now, I hear you say this is not as easy a decision as it sounds. It does depend, of course on what you are trying to achieve, so you will need to refer back to your aims (which you will have agreed before you started...). However, I urge you to consider how these decisions multiply up over a number of primary care practices. For a leadership team who have spread as their goal this is an important consideration. There is a real dilemma here between the *number* of patients and the extent and depth of the total *impact*. The tension between these two also drives the type and timing of solution that gets designed and implemented, and then of course the **knock on consequence of its ability to be spread to others.**

When investigating the lack of impact in some programs and projects my conclusion is that the cause is a combination of the lack of prior analysis and then is closely linked to the use of Plan-Do-Study-Act (PDSA) cycles.

While this model of starting off by testing small cycles of change is incredibly useful as a means of discovering what works and also reducing the risks, thus getting people engaged in the process, it does encourage the bypassing of the population of impact focus unless the project leader and team are very disciplined.

You'll have figured by now that this main issue is the Pareto Effect; that the minority of causes or inputs, leads to the majority of effects or outputs. So fancy that. This may mean that we can work on a small part of our system and get the maximum benefit. What it also means is that we might have been working on large parts of our systems and not getting much benefit at all. Why would we do that? Because often it is an easy way forward to get a quick fix, to appear to be taking action - and that is why we call this the low hanging fruit syndrome.

Picking the apples, plums and pears from the orchard in our back garden is always fraught with difficulty and temptation. The problem with crawling along the lower branches is they eventually break off under your own weight if you "go out on a limb". And the best fruit always seems at the top of the tree – just out of reach, where you have to take risks to get at it. In the end, each year we have to balance our actions to maximise the amount of produce from each tree while minimising the wastage, sharing our fruit with the birds and bees, avoiding any injury to ourselves and not causing any damage to the trees. It's a balancing act.

As with all balancing acts, when you know a bit how the system works you can manipulate it. When it comes to projects and the spread of good practice I have come across some "cheat" methods. For instance I know how to get good results for projects. All I have to do, or recommend, is to go for the low hanging fruit (or keep quiet about the population of impact – the difficult target groups). One way to look good (in the short term) is to go for these easy groups and get great results, though I know that when they all get added up, across a community (like in a spread program) the overall impact (long term for the organisation and for patient care) may not be significant.

Now there is another facet to this issue which demonstrates both the importance of the Pareto effect as well as some other technicality around the way we have come to use numbers in many of our improvement projects. If we remember, the whole point of what we're looking at here is to understand why good ideas don't spread. Well, let's look at a waiting time example.

Say a hospital aims to reduce the length of time a patient has to wait for an elective knee surgery from 90 days to 45 days. Currently it has 100 patients waiting and the variation for the past year is very stable at no more than plus or minus 10 in any one month. So, the leadership team sets the improvement team a target of 80% of patients to meet the 45 day target 95% of the time.

Immediately the improvement project leader will be spending a great deal of time working out how to make this calculation work and how to optimise the denominator and nominator of this target to his benefit. Many project leaders and teams become experts at contextualising targets and ensuring redesign work is highly specific to their environment. The successful change they do eventually make may not be the same ones that may work in another hospital to achieve the same target for precisely this reason. It would be much easier and more positive for the improvement team to be working in whole numbers and to be designing a solution to look at the whole 100 patients for the 45 day target. That way they will also be encouraged to seek within that group which of the 100 patients, because they will fall into population of impact categories, will best be served most appropriately. By doing detailed Pareto analysis upfront on their whole, they will learn to assess their system imbalances and also discover more information and knowledge about the predictability in their system. This is nearly always not what is expected, quite often counter-intuitive and can best be discovered by data analysis. This is the crux of good Pareto analysis that works with numbers and not percentages and averages.

One other advantage of working with actual numbers is it helps to engage the team members and wider group. Aims and goals like the one above may make sense to managers, however, to many clinical staff who deal with "whole people" percentages and averages have little direct meaning. To be able to count the number of people whose lives have been saved or improved is very rewarding. Or to count the amount of medication errors reported, or the amount of money saved this week on this ward by not throwing away drugs – all contributes to sense of purpose and meaning underlying the improvement work.

What has this got to do with spreading good practice? I've seen great examples like the few mentioned above where there has been spontaneous adoption. People like to see what others are doing and if it appears to be working well and it is being talked about then they'll have a go too. And that has got to be an easy way to get an idea spread around an organisation. I have very few examples of people telling me how they have spontaneously adopted something like reducing errors by 95%, or saving 80% of our medicines budget each week. In comparison, I do have examples of spontaneous and rapid adoption of good practice where the aims have been expressed in terms of saving £xx/$xx medication wasted each week on the ward, or y less administrative hours spent per week due to reduced medication errors on the ward.

So the challenge of the population of impact is to find that small group on which to test out our changes, right from the beginning, knowing this is the group where we intend to make the most impact, not where we expect to have the most successful change. Successful change does not necessarily mean useful improvement nor does it mean easy spread, as we have already seen from pilotitis.

SUGGESTED TREATMENT

Depending on the topic on which you are working the recovery from this condition is fairly straightforward once you have recognised you have a problem and are committed to resolve it.

Do the analysis.

Depending on what you are trying to achieve, work out, in detail, using the actual numbers, which population will have the most impact. You may have to cut your data a number of ways. Chart it using a Pareto chart (if you don't know how to do a Pareto chart – do an Internet search to find out – basically it looks like a histogram except it is discrete data rather than data over time). It's also important that you chart your data so you can see the *pictures* that it throws up. There is nothing more intimidating or disheartening than rows of figures. Make sure that whichever way you cut your data you are working with the large chunks of population and if you're not, then you understand why you aren't.

Spread is about impacting the population, about moving an idea that works, across a large number of people. Work out whether and how you are making an impact for that large population. If necessary make the appropriate changes to your project work and make them now.

On a more dynamic level, PDSA cycles are a great change process, especially for the start of a project. However, an even better methodology is the broader Improvement Model (please see further reading for more details) which has the addition of three questions to PDSAs

1. What are you trying to achieve?

2. How will you know you've made a difference?

3. What changes can you make?

As a minimum, ensure teams are using the Improvement Model as this will keep a proper focus. If it were me, I would enhance the second question and rewrite it as "How will you know you've made an impact?" as that will force not just the measurement approach, but also some discussion at team meetings about the concept of impact.

PREVENTING OCCURRENCES

Define the aims for your improvement work clearly at the outset, with impact in mind. You'll be surprised but I do find large programs that have no clear answer to the question "What do we want to achieve?" and that also means they have no way to measure their progress. We'll see later that even spread programs need measurement, so even at the basic improvement project level there needs to be this starting point.

Carry out a *population of impact analysis* before starting any improvement project and specifically one that has a spread intention. From small actions, large impact – both depth and breadth can occur. This is important both at a strategic and operational level. It can be done at a systems level, organisational level as well as very specific project level; with each level contributing to the impact whole.

A common and very effective improvement spread methodology is the Breakthrough Collaborative designed by the Institute for Healthcare Improvement (Cambridge, USA www.ihi.org), and I recommend it – please see further reading for more details. One useful step I have learned is to add in a diagnostic step before the first Learning Session as part of the prework phase to ensure sufficient analysis is done to discover the population of impact. In a complex topic this can take some extra weeks as teams develop the detailed assessments, data, pareto analyses and histograms.

PROGNOSIS

If caught in time and appropriate diagnostic action taken the outlook is very good.

FURTHER READING

Institute for Healthcare Improvement www.ihi.org for more information and training on the Breakthrough Collaborative Series.

Koch, Richard., The 80-20 Principle, Nicholas Brearley Publishing, London, 2003; Excellent introduction covering the broad principles in an easy read with some useful examples.

Langley, G., Nolan, K., Nolan, T., Norman ., Provost L., The Improvement Guide, Jossey-Bass, 1996; Covers the essential basics with examples from outside healthcare.

Nelson, G., Batalden, P. & Ryer, . Clinical Improvement Action Guide, Joint Commission, 1998; This is the standard and most comprehensive text for any improvement team in healthcare. It is a most practical workbook, written by practitioners who know their stuff.

Chapter 3

Outbreak of Idea Bias

PRESENTING SYMPTOMS

- You got funding or sponsorship for a project on the basis of implementing an identified and specific solution

- There is overwhelming enthusiasm and support for a single idea or solution, regardless of the diagnosis, data or context

- Only one solution or idea will be considered, for political, Political, hierarchical, ego, authoritarian or influence reasons

- You are desperate to get your idea adopted by a large group but it seems to have got stuck after being adopted by only a very small number of people

DESCRIPTION

The stars of the show at "The Apothecary" in Fredericksburg, Virginia USA are the leeches. Dressed in the period, the curators of this museum transport you back to the late 1800's and frighten the young and old, large and small with their tales of amputations, teethpulling and blood letting. Over two centuries ago blood letting, using leeches and lances was good practice for many ailments. Then it went out of fashion. Recently the use of blood letting – and leeches - is coming back into use with some trials heralding many benefits.

Everett Rogers brought us useful work with his "Diffusion of Innovations". The limitations of some of this theory we'll cover in a later chapter. However, much of the detail of this work is often overlooked such as his research on the *innovation bias*. This has been replicated and investigated by many others. His research suggested that as many as two thirds of innovations are biased to some extent, for instance by marketing, and are often not the most effective and efficient solution.

For example, the keyboard on which I am typing this script is a *qwerty* keyboard yet it is proven that a more efficient one is the *dvorak* version. This better one never took off in the marketplace so we are all left with something less superior. Technology is often left to these power battles – VHS/BETA video recorders suffered similarly and we currently have debates around DVD formats.

The same power and influence dynamics appear in healthcare when it comes to the spread of good practice. I've seen reports and reviews with sentences like "It was a best practice but the others wouldn't adopt it", "It was what was needed but it didn't spread", "The chosen model wasn't implemented by all teams", "Although it was the best practice as identified by the expert panel, the teams implemented different variations".

Another concern I have is the dominance of thought that *"good theory = good practice"*. For example, I often encounter groups that get together to design in clinical guidelines. They do this around tables using a collection of "evidence". Sometimes this is from a range of practices and my question here is whether *"good practice + good practice + good practice = best practice"*. The question is whether different contexts can be added together. So often I see teams struggle to implement the theories and put them into practice. This becomes more difficult if the guidelines are very specific. If they are left at a conceptual level with clear aims and goals then they are easier to reinvent locally. However the temptation to impose ideas appears to be quite strong and this, I believe – my evidence in the past few years – is one of the constraints in the spread of good ideas at a local level.

So what is going on when people push their own ideas on others? I have found various levels of idea bias, with different degrees of scariness and differing consequences.

An *individual* can press their idea and get away with it due to their strength of charisma, authority and influence.

A *project team*, usually based round an individual's idea may end up developing a very strong solution with well evidenced benefits for that team. So what's wrong with this I hear you ask? Well, nothing for that team. However, when it comes to spread, it may be very difficult for another team in a different context to achieve similar or even nearing similar benefits - they may even have a dis-benefit if they adopt the change. I have found little in the published literature about these dis-benefits though in practice many teams report disadvantages as the reasons for not adopting various practices or for stopping the practice altogether. Also, in many cases there are limited evaluations of the impact of large scale spread programs to assess their appropriateness and efficiency as well as knock-on impact and consequences.

An *organisation* may take on and promote a specific model or concept. They may cross promote this to others. If they have significant influence in their marketplace they may bias the group to the detriment of diversity of development of alternatives. We know from systems theory that diversity is important for sustainability so in any marketplace eventually there needs to be in operation some form of diversity and element of competition. Through this the participants in the marketplace can make decisions and choices, and continue to adapt and grow.

Nature herself is extremely wasteful in the way millions of seeds are produced to ensure the survival of the species. Credit card issuer Capital One apparently conducts thousands of experiments each year with the aim of discovering a few profitable products and services. It knows that many experiments will turn out to be useless. What they know is how little they know and therefore the only way to get a good idea is to gets lots of them and to test them out.

When I wrote *scariness* above, I was referring to the frightening prejudices that single-minded groups can have when pushing their good ideas on others. The resistance they meet is hardly surprising.

Good ideas spread, and history from the marketplace suggests that those that do are more likely to succeed in the longer term than those that don't spread. Some great ideas get drowned out by the noise of bad ideas. So, as a potential adopter, do what you can to differentiate between good ideas and bad ideas and be cautious about the contribution of noise in the system.

How do we differentiate between good and not so good ideas? I often hear individuals and teams say "that person is resistant to change". Well, one way of looking at that person is to say they are defending their own perspective, and maybe they are defending their position for a good reason. It is possible they have an excellent reason for not changing. Who is it to say that the "new" idea we are proposing is a good idea? The predominant perception that every "innovation" or proposed good practice is a good one, is, I believe, one to be cautious about. Every change comes with some consequences and needs to be thought about. Especially in complex systems where the outcomes are often emergent and cannot be fully predicted. Some of the "resistors" have good points of view that need to be taken into account and may actually strengthen the change if they are taken into account. The potential adopters are often the experts whose experience is critical to the implementation process. It may mean the "innovation" needs adapting – for the better. This is particularly the case when good ideas move from the very early pilot stage through to the more mainstream phase in organisations.

So far I have dealt mostly with the case of the single "my idea" as in my experience this is the most difficult problem to deal with and the one which most frequently holds up the spread of good practice. Sometimes you may encounter the situation where you have a glut of good ideas and competition between them. This is probably a good thing – lucky you! Test as many as possible.

SUGGESTED TREATMENT

So you are in the midst of one of those projects which are all about spreading someone's special good idea – I've been there too. It's a tough one as although it looks like a fabulous piece of good practice for some reason not everyone seems to want to adopt it. Depending on what stage you are at, here are some ideas for you. You'll have to use your common sense to work out which ones might be most appropriate for you to use right now:

- Carry out an analysis of the good practice and work out how it might be adapted. Draw up a neat (and very short) guide on its adaptability and publicise this. Help others see how it has previously been adapted. Reward those who have generated adaptations. Praise them and tell others how much you value them.

- A mid project review of progress is a good time to be looking at your solution again and its effectiveness. Many "innovations" are spread on the basis of the initial idea (and we have covered many of the issues with pilotitis in the first chapter). As they begin to spread, or if the spread process is not going to plan, then a good place to start is to review the *what*, the "innovation". So often the blame of lack of adoption is put on the adopters or their context when in my experience much of issue is around the good practice itself. What may be considered a good idea by one person or group, may not by another.

Maybe what is being described or communicated is being done so in a very limited manner? Maybe in too broad a way to be useful? Perhaps the good idea is now out of date? How relevant it is to the adopting population? Bring together a *Critical Friends* review group and spend time testing out the breadth and depth of your change package before you progress any further.

- Consider joining a validated benchmarking group. Or if one doesn't exist then create it. One excellent example of benchmarking that I admire is that of the Swedish Quality Registers. These are clinically focused and were initially led by clinicians. The ownership of the data and the response and credibility of the reports is good. They have also had an impact on the quality of care. There is nothing quite like discovering where your own performance stacks up in terms of outcome, and then to find out what it is other people are doing to achieve a better performance. However, the proviso here is to approach any copying activity with care and to ensure you take into account differences in context.

- Test some alternative ideas. This is a good option in the early stages of the project, though you can do this at any time. Even if you are mandated to implement a single idea, if you are using PDSA cycles as a method of encouraging a change in behaviour then testing slightly different ideas is easy. This way you can also discover what might not work for you, which is incredibly useful. Testing new ideas broadens the horizons of the project team and may help keep them interested and enthusiastic about the change process. This testing process, if you can make it explicit, is about helping you develop and grow your own thinking and analytical practices.

- In his book "Purple Cow", Seth Godin suggests that one of the problems that occurs is when products are created "for everybody" such that they end up targeting "nobody" because they are so generic. Has that happened to your good idea? In the Crossing the Canyon chapter we'll go into detail about how to handle this, however, the first step is to ensure your good idea or good practice is sufficiently targeted on a niche area or a specific population so as to be relevant to their context.

- A radical approach is to test how much of the idea, of the good practice, can be implemented by the user or client. Try and see it through the eyes of the end-user, and better still, redesign it entirely through their perspective, with them picking up more of the process. This may broaden and deepen the viewpoint. For example, a project to reduce the incidence of falls in a hospital may come up with a number of very creative solutions to test by involving patients in the process. Their experiences may differ from the perceptions of staff. What staff may report as "good practice" may thus be quite different from the ideas of patients.

PREVENTING OCCURRENCES

If you have a single solution in mind and are very clear about what is required then I recommend that you carry out a good old fashioned rollout implementation project, and not what has become a "spread" project. What is the difference? Well, an implementation project is a top down, hierarchical program that takes a known issue and uses classic project management techniques across existing organisational structures to implement the changes. It does not create new meetings or complicated new initiatives. It is excellent for things like safety alerts, and also for some evidence based guidelines that do not require significant behavioural changes. This method also enables efficient performance management of the adoption process.

If the management implementation process is not an appropriate option, then to reduce the possibility of idea bias and prejudice, ensure sufficient data analysis and diagnosis is completed at the start of the project. Enable customisation and adaptation of the good practice as much as possible. Involve as diverse a steering group in the creation of the local implementation to ensure the solution makes sense for them, in their own context.

PROGNOSIS

If your entire project or program is based on the implementation of a single solution with no other options available, or even encouraged, then I believe you may find some spread challenges on the horizon. Not insurmountable, though difficult. If it is genuinely a single focus issue then you do have a top down, hierarchical spread program on your hands and my suggestion is to turn it into an old fashioned implementation project.

FURTHER READING

Engaging Top Teams on the Collaborative Process is a free downloadable 22-page booklet with some of the tools from the Rollout Book and is available from the *Resources* page on www.sfassociates.biz

Fraser, Sarah W., Rolling out your project; 35 tools for healthcare improvers, Kingsham Press, 2002: This is a short book filled mostly with tools and techniques. Details available from www.sfassociates.biz

Seth Godin, Purple Cow; Transform your business by being remarkable, Penguin Books, 2005. An easy read that covers an alternative view of spread with interesting business related case studies.

Chapter 4

Myths, Methods & 'ologies

- You are presented with "The" how to guide or "The" model or "The" theory of how spread or adoption happens, especially in healthcare

- There is a constant pressure to seek a simple way or find a quick fix option or your project sponsor expects results within two to three months

- Expectations constantly outperform reality though you usually only discover this with hindsight rather than through formative measurement (see the chapter on the Measurement Deficit)

- You find yourself seduced by the theory yet the reality of business doesn't seem to match what you were taught at workshops and conferences

DESCRIPTION

"You mean the distribution curve is a different shape each time, for each different topic and each different circumstance!" Another workshop, another place, another time and another clinician who suddenly grasped a truth. "Oh, so that distribution curve we are always taught that is a normal one, is only a representative theory. Oh." Long pause while a couple of hundred brains mulled that over. And then everyone erupted in further debate at their tables. I don't know what they chose to discuss but I expect it was important to them.

Always shown as a normal distribution they had participated in an experiential exercise demonstrating how this changes under different circumstances (download instructions on how to carry out this exercise from www.sfassociates.biz resources page). For me it was obvious this was "only" a piece of theory and of course the practice is difference. But for him, as for so many others, theory was something to be taken in, studied and when presented with authority it took on a life of its own. I realised then the dangers of so much that was being "taught" in the name of "how to spread good practice" and became determined to help sort out the myths from the methodologies.

Much of this has been ensuring that I worked with participants in ways that suited their learning styles. What I have found in healthcare is that there are very few true theorists. As a result the many activist and pragmatists who prefer to operate with as little theory as possible, especially when it comes to management theory, will take small pieces of what suits them, apply it in whatever way makes sense and this is often with little regard to how that theory was developed, causing a great deal of misunderstanding in the process. For those whose professional areas rely on theory then they apply their clinical theory well. When it comes to managerial theory which has a deep research base and their knowledge comes from a short management presentation where they are unlikely to gain enough background, the likelihood of misapplication is high.

My doctorate is on the topic of how good practice spreads and most of what I learnt is how little I know. It took me into the realm of the published literature and I specifically also included the grey literature ("grey" being the term used for non-academic literature). It was project based and those who reviewed it struggled because it was non-traditional. I broke many rules in my work. I continue to read and research widely round the topic and to advance my thinking and writing beyond the realms of the currently published literature. I do this for a reason.

I am constantly asked to review papers for publication about how projects and their results have spread. I stopped agreeing to do these after they began looking like carbon copies of each other. Regardless of where they originated from in the world they referenced the same portfolio of papers. Like a virus it seemed we are unable to generate new knowledge other than to bring new case studies and slight variation on a theme.

Yet if these same authors lifted their heads and asked new questions, read a different set of literature, they would start to add to the discipline in a new way. I wondered in the last few years, what happens to the reviews of the work that doesn't spread (a little bit like asking what happens to medication research that doesn't work), and that is what led me to the research for this book.

The drive for wanting a theory to explain what has happened has turned into wanting a prescription for the future. Yet most models and theories have been developed as descriptions on what has happened in the past and they are generally unproven as predictive models – what will happen in the future. There are a few future based communication and marketing type models (like Bass Modelling) though I am not aware of these being used in healthcare to any large degree.

The most common theory that is presented at healthcare conferences and workshops, given the high ground as the main construct for explaining how good practice spreads is Rogers' "Diffusion of Innovations. (DoI)". This is a complex piece of work though usually only small parts of it are covered, most notably the communication process and the types of innovators. No doubt this model has some important and relevant features that can be applied, descriptively to any "spread" project, however, there are some significant limitations to its applicability that I believe are overlooked.

Firstly is the notion of innovation. Many healthcare "spread" projects have little to do with true innovation and are, as I've discussed in earlier chapters, straightforward management rollout projects. For example, the requirement that a simple new safety procedure be implemented is a management task. It could also be argued that implementing changes to an IT system or even implementing a registry, could be a management rollout. Indeed some of the best successes that I am aware of that are often called "spread" of registries, have been handled as a management task by their organisations – a top down, managed process – integrated into the organisation's aims and objectives.

Innovation may be required. If so it assumes something genuinely brand new is adopted by the team and there is then an element of risk. A small change or improvement is not the same as an innovation – there is a different depth of emotional connection. And this difference matters. To say *innovation* equals *improvement* and therefore the theory applies to us, I believe, does not work in practice. The Diffusion of Innovations theory is quite clear what an innovation is, yet the definition of an *improvement* is vast, with overlaps with the definition of the word *change*.

Another way to consider *innovation*, is to think of it as many different types. Different types of innovation are adopted differently. This is the subject matter for another book as it is a complex matter in itself. My argument here is that by simplifying and assuming that *innovation = improvement* and *improvement = innovation* many healthcare projects, and their subsequent publications and references, are missing and misapplying some important points.

Secondly the concept of Diffusion is incredibly important. This is diametrically opposed to dissemination. The first is a pull, the other a push in the system. One is led by the individual adopter, the other a top down, hierarchical intervention. They are different mechanisms. Diffusion is the marketing view looking back at what happened in the social system.

Dissemination is when we want something to happen so we construct a process and push to make it happen in the future.

Yes, we can learn some lessons from what happens when innovations diffuse in systems, but we can't expect the same properties of diffusion to apply when we design for dissemination.

This leads me to the third reason why I worry about the DoI theory and its applicability in healthcare. The diffusion curve is for discontinuous innovation and in my experience I have come across very few real examples in day to day practice of this happening.

We recently upgraded the Microsoft software on our computers in our office. This was a continuous innovation as the change was additive, it was small. We stayed with our PCs. Much of the functions were the same and we gained benefits for very few behavioural changes. On the other hand, if we had chosen to move to Mac computers, go wireless, change to Blackberry's, change to Sage accounting system (all on the same day) then this would count as a discontinous innovation in our office. It would require a significant change in behaviour (and stress!). The adoption rate of the various technologies would differ amongst different members of staff, according to how they felt about each of them.

So where the DoI curve can be applied *predictively* in healthcare it is specific for discontinuous innovation only i.e. where there is significant behavioural change for the adopter (not incremental).

The final concern I have with the DoI theory and how it is used, concerns the way in which the groups of adopters are used. This is not so much the fault of the theory as the way in which it is applied. However, the model does have its limitations in its language and presentation, neither of which helps its understanding and use.

Language plays an important function in how we interpret our world and I am conscious in how the use of Rogers' adopter categories appears to have generated a range of stereotypes that I hear used, and abused. The terms *innovator, early adopter, early majority, late adopter, laggard*, have, for many, turned into categories of people, with little understanding of the dynamics behind them.

The exercise mentioned at the start of this chapter is one designed to help a group understand that we are all one of these categories at some stage, hence the importance of not stereotyping anyone. Also, the terms innovator and laggard I feel are not useful in healthcare groups. As such, I have adopted others (as used by Moore), *enthusiast, visionary, pragmatist, conservative, sceptic* and I feel these are more descriptive of the real world of improvement.

For example, in the case of a project facilitator enabling a group of hospital workers to adopt new practices around the care for patients with breast cancer, she may first encounter those who are *enthusiastic* about the proposed new ideas. These individuals come on board with the project right at the start and demonstrate a great deal of initiative, excitement and creativity. They are followed by their more *visionary* colleague or two, who share their enthusiasm though temper it with a sense of idealism. They see the bigger picture. Their inspiration tends to be important and they demonstrate leadership. They are forward thinkers. They do forget about the details though and are often not interested in the finer points about the project. It is often possible to deliver the entire project with these two groups, and this is a problem as we'll see in the chapter on Crossing the Canyon.

It's when encountering the *pragmatists* in the organisation that things get caught up. This group tends to look in the other direction – backwards. They want to see the change fit into the organisation as a whole, and see its practical worth. The *conservatives* will follow what the pragmatists do and want success loaded small challenges, while the *sceptics* need to be left alone until the whole set of new ideas are well proven.

How to leverage these groups is something we'll look at later. I do feel that changing their labels and our language and how we refer to them is one of the important steps in rearranging our mental models and approach to the spread and adoption of good practice in healthcare.

SUGGESTED TREATMENT

Retain all your existing knowledge and build on it. What you already know is useful and helpful.

Next I suggest a detailed look at your own needs and an assessment of what it is you are trying to achieve. There are a number of themes falling out of this book and this chapter in particular. One is to be cautious about following one specific "how to" model or theory to the exclusion of examining any other, especially in the absence of any prior diagnosis. This is no different from you accepting treatment as a patient – you would expect a diagnosis first. And you would expect a number of options to be considered.

In your diagnosis, do consider whether you definitely have a "spread" issue or whether it is an old fashioned management rollout program. If you can get by with a top down project managed program then do it – it may achieve results quicker and more effectively. Test it out.

Read. Read around the grey literature as well as the more traditional published journals. By grey literature I mean the popular management books and regular press. Read outside your industry. Visit outside your industry. Network outside your industry. Find out what others are doing and learn from them. In the world of improvement and quality management healthcare has traditionally followed industry and it seems a shame this should continue in the "spread" topic, especially as healthcare is carrying out some of the largest change programs and can essentially benefit hugely if it were sufficiently courageous and were conducting double loop learning.

What's double loop learning? It's when you review your learning and ask yourself whether you are learning the right things? Are your aims and objectives the right ones? Like asking the questions "Is the concept of spreading good practice an appropriate one?", "Why does good practice not spread?" etc.

Action research and action evaluation is a decent way to develop new models and I know of a number of projects underway that are undergoing processes that will benefit from this rigour. However, I suspect many will bow to the references of traditional published literature and as such not benefit from the new thinking. I do hope they stretch and we get some new projects that will look to discover, to answer some of the unanswered and difficult questions. And do this in a practical, pragmatic way.

Publish. Let's publish new work that breaks out the virus of old models and methodologies.

PREVENTING OCCURRENCES

Funny thing is, it doesn't matter what stage I am at in my various diets and weights, those "one size fits all" t-shirts never seem to fit me. The lesson I've learnt is always to try my clothes on before purchasing them, to test them out, and to know that different makes will have different sizing and that not all will suit me. I need to shop around to find out what will work best for me.

Maybe that is the story here for keeping the myths at bay. We do need models to help us make sense of our world and we'll wrap them in methodologies. The discipline is to avoid the temptation or seduction of the first offer and to read, listen, connect, network – do what you can – to find the most appropriate and satisfying solution that meets your own needs.

PROGNOSIS

The domination of "Diffusion of Innovation" as a synonym for "spread of good practice" will continue for as long as editors of journals and reviewers continue to accept for publication healthcare orientated papers and articles that continue the biased interpretation based. The same goes for those who perform major research and projects and evaluations. The DoI work has a great depth and is often misinterpreted and misapplied in its use. Used appropriately it can be helpful. Otherwise handle with care.

I suspect it will take some years for healthcare publications and methodologies to make the leap that is currently to be evident in the grey literature and in the private sector.

FURTHER READING

Jeffrey Pfeffer & Robert Sutton, Hard Facts, Dangerous Half-Truths, and Total Nonsense: Profiting from Evidence-Based Management, Harvard Business School Press, 2006. A brilliant response to the fads and fashions that will help you in your critical reading.

Rogers, E, The Diffusion of Innovations, 1995 The Free Press; This is the definitive version of what you need to read if you really want to know the *detail* of the theory. This book is really quite readable.

Chapter 5

Crossing the Canyon (a.k.a. the Deep Depresson...)

PRESENTING SYMPTOMS

- You've managed to spread results to 20%-25% of an identified population but then ground to a halt

- Adoption rates have slowed down and you've got your sponsor or management chasing you to produce results quickly

- The solution you started with now doesn't seem to be the right one; everyone wants to change it before they take it on

DESCRIPTION

After seven years of working on spread programs I have come across three main types of spread plans which are produced at the start of a spread program. They tend to fall into the following categories:

a) "Tipping Point Optimism" (TPO) – "When we reach the tipping point of 16% then everyone will automatically adopt the good practice". This comes from the DoI theory and is, in my opinion, a mistaken belief and a misapplication of the theory (inappropriately predictively assuming a normal discontinuous innovation curve for their good practice)

b) "Single Idea Bias" (SIB) – "This is such a good idea it suits everyone" or "Everyone needs to do this exactly the same way" – or something similar, which means this is best as a management rollout plan and not as a complex spread plan.

c) "Complex Communications" (COCO) – This is a plan made up of very complex and varied communications strategies, with or without supporting structures.

All of these plans, and combinations thereof, lack something, though the last version has more redeeming features that the first two. I no longer see very many of the first version though it does occasionally crop up. The problem is not so much in the plans but in the fact they do not address the root problem – the fact that in nearly all active, purposeful, spread programs that I have come across, most have great difficulty encouraging adoption beyond 20-25% of the targeted population. This appears regardless of the size of target population, the context and the type of solution.

The dynamic at play here is a combination of "pilotitis" and "idea bias" and the domination of the idea that one single solution will work across and in all contexts and with all populations. However, evidence suggests a different strategy is required to achieve your goals in the target market.

The key phase here is "achieve your goals in the target market" as opposed to "spread the good practice to a target population". Reducing the time patients wait for elective knee operations, or improving the quality of care for patients with diabetes, can be achieved in a number of different ways, in differing contexts, by applying different good practices to varying degrees, at different times.

Let's see how this can play out. I'll use myself as an example first. As a confirmed PC user I have avoided any Apple Mac products as these are generally incompatible with my range of PC Windows products. My old MP3 player needed replacing – I purchased a very early version, being somewhat ready to accept technological risks. I was adamant not to purchase an Apple IPOD as I was convinced it would not be compatible with my other systems. I did not trust it. It was too risky (although I continued to purchase other techytype things and try them out). However, eventually I was won over when I realised the IPOD has nearly 70% of the market and when I wanted a Video version it was going to be the best bet. Also there were a lot of accessories for it so it seemed to be the market leader. I eventually purchased an IPOD 5th generation. Some people see me with it, amongst all my other techy-gear and think I am continuing my "risky" behaviour, but far from it. When it comes to the IPOD, I was well in the norm, waiting for the market leadership to show its hand and to demonstrate that it would work with my office systems. I am much the same when it comes to mobile phones.

From the Apple perspective they had to work hard to get me to adopt it. They were on their 5th iteration of the product. It had developed way beyond the first model they produced in terms of features, reliability and market acceptability (including accessories and how others were allowed to customise it). They had moved through a number of different niche markets before they reached me. They developed their market share by soaking up markets niche by niche.

So how might this example transfer to healthcare? Think about how a new clinical guideline appears to work well in one hospital with good results and you want the whole of a health economy to adopt its use so a large number of patients can benefit from its use. Well, often this guideline is like the 1st generation IPOD. It works well for those who invented it, specifically for their use and it felt good at the time. However, things move on over time, new ideas come along and other people have different ideas. Maybe a 2nd generation gets developed and this does help adoption a little bit and this is how come adoption reaches the 20 – 25% level. What industry has learnt, like for the IPOD, is that **continuous adoption requires an almost continuous improvement process**. Note that this is more than a small bit of customisation here and there. It can mean significant redevelopment.

This is not a linear process. It is linked to the groups of people as identified in the research discovered by Rogers and we renamed in an earlier chapter. The step changes in a good practice occur as each tranche of people are met, as we move from the initial *enthusiasts* to the *visionaries* who will most likely want some small changes to the good practice. They may want changes to go along with their more strategic and purposeful ideas. The biggest barrier comes when we meet the *pragmatists*. The first two groups are forward looking while the next three look rearwards. This is where we find the canyon – between the visionaries and the pragmatists.

The pragmatists – like me and my IPOD – need convincing that the good idea won't collapse the systems that they hold dear and protect. Pragmatists serve a useful purpose in organisations; without them holding structures together, in times of change, chaos may reign. They need proof that the good practice works as a cohesive whole, functions without error, is reliable and is well evidenced. This is a good group to take on a field trip to visit the place where the good practice is already working well (unlike the enthusiasts and visionaries who may find this sort of trip patronising and boring).

SUGGESTED TREATMENT

Bridging the canyon and helping pragmatists (*conservatives* and others will follow later) adopt requires a great deal more than communication programs and in some cases more than a management rollout program, if there are insufficient carrot – stick / reward – disincentive measures that can be put in place.

There are three key strategies to bridge the canyon (a) re-develop and refine the good practice (b) use a niche implementation strategy (c) encourage diversity in application.

Most industries have a "Product Development" department who acknowledge and work within a product lifecycle pattern, and this is closely linked to the marketing process, and also research if there is one. There is no assumption that products have an infinite life – far from it. Instead, refinements are continually under development, with their marketing and target population in mind.

How does this fit with the improvement culture within healthcare? Once an improvement idea has been discovered, it is often then identified to be spread to others, in the original form, maybe with allowances for local reinvention. Some measurement is put in place to check implementation happens within, for example 12 – 18 months.

Another ways to approach this may be to focus on the results that the improvement provides and measure those (rather than the implementation of the good idea itself). Secondly, during the implementation phase to expect only say 25% to adopt the original idea and while this is happening, have a development team work on refining the original idea to make it more acceptable to pragmatists and to test this out in a variety of "pragmatist" conditions.

This leads me to the niche approach. Rather than attempt to spread a good idea to a whole target population, in order to make it more acceptable to the pragmatists, demonstrate its worth by saturating one area. This could be a whole ward, a whole department, an organisation, a health economy – it depends on the size of your spread strategy in the first place. Time and time again, the market place has proven that taking niche areas as wholes is preferable to scatter attempts and thinly spread sectors of adopters where word of mouth is difficult to motivate and where it is difficult to demonstrate capacity and capability.

Think of an example of a clinical guideline. If your aim is to have it adopted by a whole health economy then using this niche approach you would start by working in one area, aiming for saturation in that area, before you attempted to spread the word in other areas.

Finally we have the concept of diversity. One of the reasons the IPOD has taken off is because there is a whole range of accessories that have been developed for it. Many of these are not official Apple ones. By making some of its technology available (but not all), some items have been able to be made for sale by other suppliers. This win-win relationship has been important to its success. Very exclusive products often find it difficult to compete. Similarly, think about complex good practices where you need special and expensive training courses where only trainers with specific licenses can give them. This can slow down potential adoption of good ideas and their benefits.

The focus of this chapter is the "canyon" that appears between the visionaries and the pragmatists, somewhere after 20% of adoption. Other than money and the carrot/stick approach, the best high level strategies I have come across to resolve this are those I have listed above. In the minutiae of facilitating change, then there are, of course, many other ideas you can use.

PREVENTING OCCURRENCES

This phase is also known as the *Deep Depression*, or the opposite of the natural Tipping Point, as things don't seem to take off on their own, instead everything grinds to a halt and unless you push hard nothing seems to happen at all.

Know that there is little evidence to suggest single ideas are adopted by the masses in a push strategy unless there are carrots & sticks attached. If you have a SIB plan then be aware of limitations. If your plan is one of optimism, TPO, then you may be one of the very few who have a genuine discontinuous innovation and some special circumstances that make this work. If this happens then please publish your results and report it widely as there are few known.

Generally, be prepared to be flexible in your approach and this means changing your good practice over time – continuously - and in different contexts, with different groups, in a purposeful and planned way. I think the canyon is always there so expect to build a bridge of some form.

PROGNOSIS

With knowledge, forethought and foresight – excellent.

Without – please re-read the opening line of this book!

FURTHER READING

Moore, G. A. Crossing the Chasm – Marketing & Selling Disruptive Products to Mainstream Customers, 1991 and **Inside the Tornado – Strategies for Developing, Leveraging and Surviving Hypergrowth Markets, 1995,** both **HarperBusiness Essentials.** Both of these books are essential reading for anyone considering spread programs. They feel far more relevant to much of the work we are doing in healthcare, even though they are private sector orientated. They push the boundaries and show the way. Though interesting to note they are not recent publications – their message is still very current for those who have yet to get up to speed with what is going on outside healthcare.

Chapter 6

Neurally Intelligent Network Influencers (nini's)

PRESENTING SYMPTOMS

- Some messages, and not always the ones you want, spread round your system like wildfire, yet others appear to have no effect whatsoever

- You know of the theory of "opinion leaders" but don't seem to be able to make it work for you in practice

- You find it difficult to get anyone interested in your project or on the spread phase of an initiative

- After a departmental or organisational reorganisation you're not sure who to contact about how to get anything done, irrespective of job titles

DESCRIPTION

When the first Diffusion of Innovation (DoI) research studies were completed I wasn't even born. Fancy that! By the time the fundamental pieces of research were completed that created the discipline, TV and traditional advertising was in its heigh-day and the internet was unheard of by the majority of the world. The theory is relatively unchanged since the mid-1990's. Since Rogers' seminal work was first published in 1984 people born in that year are over 22 years old and have lived lives that bear no recognition to those described or known in the research contained in the book. They are called

Digital Natives to distinguish them from *Digital Immigrants* – those who have had to get to grips with the multi-media world we now inhabit. These young adults, today's new opinion leaders, use, apply and are influenced by media in a way that bears no recognition to the research covered in DoI. In fact this may apply to many older adults who have embraced these newer technologies.

The concept of an "opinion leader" – someone whose behaviour we copy – is very complex and part of our social structure. In the days when these structures and networks were more formal and dependent on certain social criteria and where geographic co-location was important they were easier to analyse and plot. Even then they were an emerging and constantly adapting process, and in today's fast paced society I suggest they are emerging in a different manner.

Today we have the complexity of virtual networks which are part of many people's lives to varying extents. For some this is nothing more than the odd email and glance though the search engine. Others may spend some hours each day connecting with their friends and business colleagues through various social and business networking websites. One of the most famous is *Myspace* – initially for teenagers, though now used by all ages. Business networking is conducted using systems such as *LinkedIn* and I am a member of *eCademy.com* which has some extraordinary features for helping connect individuals. There are ranking systems that can specifically denote factors such as "opinion leadership", you can see who is connected to whom and check the frequency of your own contacts etc. For businesses that want to figure out whom to tap into when trying to pitch a product or close a sale then there are products like *Spoke* and *Visible Path*. If you want to connect up to a hundred people in a conference call over the internet then you can do so on a *Skypecast* – free of charge.

By the time you read this – these will all probably be old hat, having been replaced by newer and more up to date versions, such is the way of technology. My point is, there are growing sophisticated means and methods for both operating and measuring social networks. Which are you using?

We are all influenced by others and in different ways. So often I encounter project teams who are looking for the single opinion leader who will carry their message for them through their organisation. The practice, and prevailing theory, is this is an unrealistic expectation. Let's look at some of the issues.

If you wanted advice before you purchased a new fruit tree for your garden, to whom would you go? If you were buying a new computer for home use, whose opinion would you canvass? And for a digital camera? Are these different people? In the majority of cases I expect so.

When it comes to the topics of improvement projects, clinical evidence into practice initiatives and other change management programs, this sensitivity is important. The clinician who looks to a colleague for advice on diagnosing patients with potential colorectal cancer will likely look to a different colleague for advice on lung cancers. Within those specialities they may further "specialise" their opinion leadership, and probably do this quite unconsciously.

This unconscious influencing process is a continually adaptive process. I named this chapter *neurally intelligent network influencers* because that is how I perceive our social network systems to work. They operate as a neural network, sparking off, intelligently, and with no hierarchy. This idea of no hierarchy is important. In the DoI research of old there was work which indicated that opinion leaders were of a higher social status, had above average communication skills and had access to superior information. Well, I am not sure that is still relevant in today's fast moving and technologically driven society.

If I want to find out how to use the features of my recordable DVD player I am likely to ask someone under the age of 14. I took up SMS / text messaging after I got jealous watching my mother and my aunt doing it for months. I learn about new clothing fashions from a trip to the hairdresser and am most likely to adopt these ideas after I've had my haircut! If I need to know about Home Care Models I will get onto my contacts in New York, using the phone or internet. I am influenced by all types of people.

The same applies to many improvement projects I've seen at work in healthcare organisations. I've seen much non-peer driven influencing occur. For example, at a large chronic care conference I was struck by how many attendees were as interested in the discussion and debate from the group as they were from the presenter. Many times these participants were not their peers. Some of the comments on the evaluation forms mentioned that the facilitated discussion after the presentations was what they found most useful and I would then expect this to be the most influential part of the conference for those who attended.

Peer influencing is still important, though in the right circumstances and context. Cross peer influencing I expect happens far more frequently than the formal research I believes give credit. Also the changes in opinion leadership are far more subtle and adaptive than many organisations expect. Used to hierarchical structures based on roles and job titles, I have found many project teams expecting identified "champions" to operate like social network opinion leaders and being disappointed when they don't. Mining social networks tends to strip them of their value leaving their participants suspicious, developing new and underground networks deeper and further away from prying eyes.

In our work structures the conditions for managing information and knowledge are changing rapidly. How work is done has changed dramatically and this is also challenging how training is done – or can be done. For example, is there a need for knowledge based training when nowadays workers of all levels and types have their own networks of people and information sources to help them find and make use of critical information sources when needed. Social applications like blogs, instant messaging, online project portals, collaborative authoring sites, social bookmarking, online resources and other tools are all being called into use on a just-in-time basis.

In activities that are largely virtual then the opportunities for removing the peer related barriers are increased. I am thinking about large scale change programs such as virtual collaboratives. Here we may have groups of twenty, thirty and maybe even seventy or so teams all connected together using technology, negating the need to travel to a common face-to-face venue. Some collaboratives I have worked with use a hybrid of both virtual and face-to-face working, combining the benefits of both.

Leveraging nini's across virtual networks can be complex and does require an infrastructure to support it. Or as a minimum vigilance about the phenomenon and then some flexible encouragement of networks after discerning what might be possible in any given setting. One of the complaints I often hear is "no-one uses the listserv" or "virtual working doesn't work". Well, in the early days of project management or improvement facilitation there was a significant amount of effort put into the appropriate skill building to ensure that individuals had the capability and capacity to do what was required of them. I believe the same is required for virtual working. At the time of writing this book, many traditional improvement programs and organisers have yet to make the leap to include social networking technologies in their virtual working. For many it is not a natural shift. Training in virtual moderation and facilitation is a requirement. The educational techniques to run online events are quite different from those required for face-to-face events. Transferring from one to another does not guarantee success.

Similarly, expecting the face-to-face nini to operate the same way as the virtual nini is unrealistic. They may be one and the same, they may be different people. One important factor to consider, is to remember that spread is about communication - in that I believe Rogers was right - and to consider just how virtual, as in technology, communication is impacting your context. If you think it is not yet impacting, then ask yourself – why not?

SUGGESTED TREATMENT

This has bothered me more than most of the issues that have been raised in this book. Mostly because of the elitist connotations that tend to go with the term "opinion leader" as originally defined by Rogers and in much of the consequential research. Yet in all my practical experience, what I see happening is both peer driven influence and cross-peer influence as well as influence across the social divide almost purely based on adoption need (pull). With these factors in mind, if you are interested in stimulating the spread and adoption process then the following ideas may help you:

- Whilst recognising that technology is not the be-all and end-all it is a crucially important factor as we move towards the end of the first decade of the 21st Century. If you are working on improvement projects in healthcare and are not engaged in the latest quality improvement techniques then it would be useful to get up to date – similarly with spread. Spread is dominated by how communication works. And communication nowadays is dominated by how technology works. Get it!

- Find out who in your organisation is up to date with the latest communication technology. You need to know enough about it to know what questions to ask. Do your internal systems allow access to the main social networking sites? Do you encourage their use? Can you use them in any way for your projects?

- What communication support do you provide specifically to your known nini's? They need extra in terms of access to a wide variety of media type and extra content. How can you help them make contact with others and extend their own social networks? The larger their social networks, the better it is for you.

- If your organisation has recently been through a reorganisation or merger, what can you do to help teams recreate their social fabric? They will have some existing networks that may need support and some help in establishing new ones. The better support you can provide, the better nini's can work. Strong networks can provide for strong influencing processes.

- What group networking sites do you use for your improvement projects? How do you encourage nini behaviour in your projects? Do use products such as *Microsoft Sharepoint* or *Webex Weboffice* as project central system for your projects to help with social networking, as well as project co-ordination?

- Do you have *listservs*? What instant messaging services are available for staff in your organisation? Which ones do they use informally? And if you think they aren't, some of them – some nini's – are using them quite effectively for their own purposes! Do you have virtual moderator classes and training courses to help those who will be working on virtual teams?

- One way to discover the nini in any group is to ask the question of any one person, "Whose opinion do you value and respect with regard x (where x is the good idea to be spread)?". I have found this quite often elicits this person's nini. I then ask this question of each person in the group. That way I can quietly create a network map and identify the personal nini's.

- A brokering model is one way to try to create opportunities to put nini's together from different departments or organisations and see if they would like to share knowledge with one another. For example, it is often difficult to extract information from these experts as they may be very reluctant to share their hard won knowledge. So by going for a brokering or collaboration type arrangement with a peer it may be less threatening and more amenable. The aim is always the spread and adoption of better ideas, knowing that there will most likely be some reinvention as well. I have see this at work with two very senior consultants who were reluctant to share any of their work yet reported afterwards that they didn't mind sharing with each other across their organisations in this, as one of them called it, respectful, way.

PREVENTING OCCURRENCES

We can't prevent nini's! Opinion leadership is in the control of other people. They operate either strongly or weakly, depending on the nini's ability associated along with the strength of the social network itself. So if you can, create an environment that nurtures networking, providing the context for nini's to flourish.

PROGNOSIS

Much of the focus of this chapter has been on technology and you may disagree with the line I've taken. So be it. However, social networking is a theory that fascinates me. Indeed it is worthy of a book on its own – if I felt it were concrete and practical enough for such a thing! When it comes to opinion leadership and how to leverage it, I find that the theory has often been oversimplified to the extent that many people get very frustrated as they cannot "make it work for them" in practice. Well, sorry about that – it's complex. The other part of understanding the theory is, what I have tried to touch on in this chapter, that it is so closely linked to communications technology, and this technology is changing at such great speed that it is difficult to keep up, which is one of the reasons why the concepts are difficult to get a handle on and to control.

So my recommendation is to take snapshots in time, work with what information and knowledge you have, knowing full well that it will adapt and change at any moment. In other words, when it comes to opinion leadership - go with the flow.

FURTHER READING

Friedman, T.L., The World is Flat. Penguin, 2005; A riveting read about the globalised world in the twenty-first century. If you haven't yet grasped the virtuality of our world this book will help you do so.

Keys & Links and Ladders; Two Games for Accelerating the Spread of Good Practice – details from www.sfassociates.biz/our shop This training pack has two experiential games, one of which is a board game, the other uses cards, which helps you work with groups to understand and spread good practice.

Experiential games to spread good practice – free downloads available from www.sfassociates.biz on the resources page.

Chapter 7

Slips, Trips & Falls

PRESENTING SYMPTOMS

- The whole project, and some of the project teams seem to lack focus and direction (*Focus*)

- Seems to take ages for anything to happen; like it takes twelve months just to get some stakeholders engaged in the process (*Engagement*)

- You start off doing PDSA cycles, then keep doing PDSA cycles, then do more PDSA cycles, and things keep changing and it seems like no-one knows when to stop tweaking things (*PDSA*)

- Or almost the opposite – you have such great results from the first pilot project that you dare not change anything in the spread phase, after all, you've been told that variation is a bad thing (*Customisation*)

- You started the spread phase of a project, with the intent to spread results to a wider audience, then with a sinking feeling, realise that maybe the problem you're having is you haven't yet achieved proper results with the first few sites (*Results*)

- You're finding that the language you use all the time is "engage", "involve", "getting over resistance" and phrases like that (*Facilitation*)

DESCRIPTION

This chapter is a hotch-potch of the miscellany of issues that come under the title of "spread" that in my experience are encountered in the spread phase of a program, yet are probably nothing to do with the traditional niche theory of the "spread of good practice" per se. These six concerns are common patterns that keep raising their head in my consultancy practice and in this chapter I shall describe each briefly, with some ideas for their resolution – in terms of and in the context of, what you probably encounter in your programs that you call the spreading of good practice.

One of the temptations when spreading good ideas as a *push,* is to encourage individuals and teams to adopt good practices with little regard to how these fit with their personal, team or organisational objectives. However, an important alignment step is to ensure an appropriate fit. This is as much a psychological process as an administrative one.

In addition, new project teams set up to spread results benefit from time spent ensuring they agree their goals and aims. They need to be able to answer the question "What are we trying to achieve" and "How will we know when we have accomplished our goal". Without a sense of purpose and focus teams are easily diverted from their task during the creative learning cycle process and team members can become demotivated. Results can become slow to materialise and sponsors impatient.

Without a clear *focus,* in the spread phase, projects can easily become distracted by one person's idea of what needs to be achieved, or one person's idea (see "outbreak of idea bias"). Engagement drops, interest wanes and it is unlikely that teams will achieve the desired results.

For some projects their centre of attention becomes how to engage others in a change process. For them the issue at hand may relate more to problems of "pilotitis". You may find yourself embarking on large communication programs or workshops where you disseminate information about the possibilities of what can be done and spend much time and money on this stage and phase of change. *Engagement* becomes an all consuming process and almost the end in itself.

One of the concerns here is the extent of engagement and this has been addressed in "crossing the canyon" – whether to engage all the stakeholders at once, or, as has been proven to be a more effective technique, to go for a more localised, niche strategy. This may enable a better balance between the engagement process and implementation, so some results can start to be achieved.

As part of this implementing strategy, one of the dilemma's that face many teams using the *PDSA* learning cycle approach is when to stop with the small test cycles and go for the big step change. What do I mean by this? One of the questions often raised by teams is when should they stop with PDSAs, how do they recognise when they have a successful change, and when should they move to a large scale implementation of this change across their wider system?

To the PDSA purist, one never stops using the PDSA approach because it is a way of learning. However, in practice, there does actually come a time when the small tests of change do need to stop and practically it is useful to consider whether to **accelerate** the change across the organisation. Note the emphasis on the word accelerate. I feel that to continue to use the PDSA process in many circumstance actually holds back the delivery of results. Let's look at an example.

You are running a project to reduce the number of hospital acquired infections (HAI's) in the hospital. You have started in your project in Ward 1 and conducted numerous test cycles and discovered three really useful changes you can implement. One of these is administrative, one is a ward design change and one is behavioural and means the clinical staff needs to do different things. Firstly it is very important that you are able to demonstrate that these changes are able to produce measurable successes so it will be important to track your progress. You may like to reduce the number of changes you are making, or at the very least, if you make any more changes, be sure you can show on a chart when another change is made, so any impact can be seen on any result.

If you have complaints about too many PDSA cycles being done and you don't know whether they are working or not then the most important question to ask is "what are the measures saying". Most times I encounter that issue I discover there are no measurements in place, just lots of people making lots of changes at whim, which is usually of no point at all – how do you know the changes are making any difference?

When you do know your changes are successful then my recommendation is to stop making changes and allow them time to bed in and prove themselves.

The next step is the spread phase and this is when you have to choose whether you are going to move to the traditional management rollout phase (see earlier chapters) or not. If you do, then integrating the results into other parts of the organisation's aims and objectives will be key.

Moving results to other parts of the organisation will most likely require some form of *customisation*. At this stage you may baulk at this believing that any variation should be frowned upon, having been taught that variation is a bad thing when it comes to quality improvement. However, the issue here is that customisation is the way in which the good idea is implemented, not in how the result or outcome is generated. For example, if your aim is to have HAI's at a certain level, then set a target and aim at that. Share the good ideas on how to achieve that. Keep the focus on the target and allow the customisation at the level of the good idea and not at the level of the target. It is achieving the target that matters.

Another of the issues that come under the "slips, trips and falls" heading is the "*no results*" category. This is when spread programs start up before the initiating teams have results they can spread to others. The whole point of a spread phase is that there is something to be spread. It can put enormous pressure on an originating team if they are still trying to come up with the goods at the same time as trying to bring along another team or teams.

Now the good news is we know that good ideas spread quicker than industry best practice (see my Spread book if you need the theory underpinning this). So in fact the originating team does not need to have perfect, well evidenced, finalised proven best practice work. In fact that would most likely hinder the adoption process. What they do need though, are some results that show they have implemented change that was, for them, better than before and then they need to be able to communicate this in simple and effective ways.

The final and very common issue holding up spread programs is one of *facilitation*. Any change process is a personal one and this demands a facilitation process. Spread is based around communication and this demands skills and abilities in addition to regular change management capabilities. I have found some project managers using mostly email to run their programs who are then surprised to find them slow to take off, without realising that if they at least added phone calls to their repertoire they could greatly improve their influencing capabilities. Also, facilitation skills are seldom taught on spread programs, the implication being they, or advanced communication skills, are not required.

SUGGESTED TREATMENT

Most of the problems sketched out above are familiar to you and I am sure you have many ways to get round them. Common sense, regular project management approaches, facilitation exercises, quality improvement tools and organisational development work will cover most of the techniques to prevent and recover from any of the issues you might encounter.

If you feel there is a lack of *focus* in your program and project work, there probably is. Take some time out and start at the top. Look at the highest level. Do you have a clear goal? Is there a purpose to your work that is clear and understandable by everyone working on the project? If not, then how can you devise one and get this message spread?

Next, do you have clear aims that can be measured so that when they are achieved everyone knows they have been achieved. For example, "x% of patients to have an A1c below 7%", "Reduce acute care hospitalisations to 23%". If you find that you are working on activities that are difficult to relate to your aims then you may need to reconsider the scope of your project, or add in some new aims such as "y% of patients to be trained in self management techniques by n date".

It is probable that when you move to the spread phase of a program you may need to revise your aims for the program to make sure that they have a good fit with the intentions of both the sponsors and the adopters.

Ensure potential adopters have space to fit aims within their own organisational or department purposes. In some programs this means they create their own set of customised objectives. It may mean something subtle such as tweaking the broader aim to read: "x% of patients registered to Dr z to have an A1c below 7% by the end of the current year", or "y% of patients registered to abc practice to be trained in z self management technique by y date" (where z self management technique specifically fits with a goal that abc practice has set itself to implement within the timeframe). The customisation of the aims like this is a psychological commitment process that teams will go through in their quality improvement process. It is both a step in focusing as well as engaging.

With regards *engagement* overall, as mentioned previously this can become an all consuming process. If your goal is to reach thousands of clinicians with the aim of changing their behaviour then your program is going to be a long term one, the first step of which will be disseminating information (push) and encouraging engagement in a number of initiatives designed to build capability and interest, such as training and audit. The temptation here is to go for the whole group and to try to engage them all in one go, falling into the *idea bias* trap and the *crossing the canyon* difficulties.

The best way that I know to approach a large group – isn't. Namely, to break it into smaller groups. However large your group is, think how to break it down into smaller potential adopter groups. If you have National groups, go Regional, or go Local; If Regional, go Organisational, then departmental, then into teams. Go for the niche market. Get one area up and running at a time. Then move onto the next. This is what builds a critical mass of **both** engagement and implementation. Even if your ultimate target is to reach the whole "market" by a certain date, this can be achieved by moving through it, small group at a time, rather than trying to start from a mass approach. The story is in the maths, and we'll touch on more about this in the measurement chapter. However, if you feel uncertain about this concept, please reread the "crossing the canyon" chapter as this is where the main issues with engagement are dealt with.

In summary, for engagement, if you feel you are getting nowhere because you are having difficulty raising the profile of the ideas behind what you are trying to achieve then have a think about how you are selling your work. One way of thinking about it is that no-one is ever interested in doing your project, they are only ever interested in having their problems solved. So how are the good ideas you are putting forward going to solve their problems? And remember that each different person, be they a nurse, a manager, a doctor, a porter, whoever, they will all want a different reason as to why they should take on the idea you are presenting to them.

Now we move onto the action and implementation phase once we have people engaged. So you are into *PDSA* cycles and wondering in the spread phase how to use them. If you have decided that teams will use them as a means of getting started with their work then let them get on with it though have the expectation that PDSAs should accelerate implementation. Accelerate means you should expect some speeding up. There should be translation or copying of ideas from the originating project and not a complete reinvention. That is the purpose of this being a spread phase. They should start with some ready idea. A bit like starting with a ready-mix cake. They can still customise it, though they have a base from which to start.

For the spread group it is very important to focus them on results and to ensure they are orientated on measurements. They may be teams that have not had the benefit of quality improvement skills training. So providing them with turnkey project management kits to help them manage their processes will be important. Without measurement it will be difficult for them to know whether they are making any progress.

These spread teams will also start to *vary* in the solutions they implement. In my experience many project managers from originating teams who are supporting spread phases are cautious about allowing variation, believing it to be wrong. As mentioned above the key here is to focus on the measurement outcome rather than the solution. Where possible allow variation in the solution. In some cases this may not be possible, such as in organisational IT systems where commonality may be preferable, or where you need common coding systems. However, some local ward systems may be quite fine, as long as the results are achieved. In some cases, exploring why there is a need to be different may be helpful, though this may be useful at a later date.

On the issue of the need to achieve *results* before moving on to the spread phase there is not much advice to add here except to either hold the spread phase until results have been achieved or to ensure results have been achieved within the expected timeframe. The alternative is to change the nature of the project to be one which includes the number of teams at the start - that is to include those intended to be in the spread phase - and then have one large original project rather than a first phase and a spread phase. Though my preference is the first one – deliver results first, then spread.

Finally we have *facilitation*. I see many presentations about the difficulties of spread or how to overcome the problems and most of them look like a "how to do facilitation or organisational development", though not with that title. So my advice here is to check whether some of the difficulties you are having are not down to traditional change management issues which can be dealt with using known tried and tested facilitation or organisational development techniques.

You will have many facilitators and OD consultants within your organisation who will be able to help you with this work, both in terms of diagnosis and support to recover. I guess what I am saying here is the problem is not a fancy one called "spread", but rather something more familiar, though not necessarily easy, where you can use regular change management techniques with which to address it.

PREVENTING OCCURRENCES

Slips, trips and falls can be prevented with awareness. The more you think about what might be going on with your program, the more you can be working to get and keep it on track.

PROGNOSIS

Just because it's called a "spread" program doesn't mean it has to be a spread type problem that is blocking your progress. Much of the time it may be something quite straightforward that needs your attention, and you definitely have the skills and capabilities to sort it out.

FURTHER READING

Scholtes, Peter, Leaders Handbook ; this is a comprehensive guide to improvement, project management and facilitation and I thoroughly recommend it. I use it when I need to be dug out of a hole! An excellent reference book and a very easy read.

Chapter 8

The Measurement Deficit

PRESENTING SYMPTOMS

- Spread plan with no measurement (what, no spread plan even!)

- Spread teams that are unaware of the number of their target audience; namely they do not know how many potential adopters they are expecting to adopt their good practice

- Uncertainly around the difference between formative and summative spread measurement and how this can help the spread process

- Spread plans based on counting push activities only with little if any focus on outcome or impact

DESCRIPTION

If you find yourself as the program manager of a spread phase and you don't have an overall plan for this phase that tells you when you expect who to have adopted what by when and what impact you expect that will have had on your system, then it becomes a little difficult to know what activities to lead.

SUGGESTED TREATMENT

I thought the best approach here would be to describe a high level spread plan for a large system, from which you can take some ideas and customise this for your own use. I have written this as a series of steps so you can see how a plan might be constructed.

Step 1: Write the single goal for your spread phase. This is the one overarching aim you are trying to achieve. Where possible it needs to be measurable, though in some cases it may not, and we can build measures at a later stage. Bear in mind, some spread phases can be huge programs. For example: "100% adoption of new guidelines for usage of alcohol hand gel by all staff in all hospital wards in x region", "Reduce acute care hospital admissions to 23% by June 2007", "Implement registries in all primary care practices by 2010".

Step 2: Write a short description of the project, indicating the existing good practice and who the demonstrator sites are. This need be no more than a couple of paragraphs. Note any special needs or situations.

Step 3: This is the measurement plan. There are many ways to construct your measures and to do this you will need to know at least two pieces of information:

1) The number of potential adopters; and this needs to be in detail. If you are focusing on organisations, then count the organisations as well as the number of individuals within them, and try to work out the different types of people within them. If you are targeting 24,000 clinicians then you need to know that. If you are targeting 6 hospitals, with 78 wards and 984 clinical staff then you need to know that too.

2) The key impact measure. Often also called the outcome measure. Though note I use the word *impact* to make sure this is a true outcome measure and that it drives you to connect with the population of focus. You need at least one measure that will track whether the work your teams are delivering is making a difference.

Now with the above you can begin to construct your measurement plan. There are three parts to this: (a) Engagement Measures, (b) Process Measures, and (c) Impact / Outcome Measures.

Why are these three types of measurements important? Think of them each as pools of adopters. The impact pool is an important one – this is what ultimately matters. The amount of impact, the amount of adopters, ultimately comes from the amount of adopters who actually go through the process of change. They come from the pool of those in the process measures. And those in the process pool come from those who have been engaged. So you want a large pool of those who are engaged. So you want very many people engaged, lots of people going through the process, so you can get an impact. If you are not keeping tabs on what is happening up front in the spread process, it is difficult to influence the impact.

Engagement Measures are ways of checking whether you are reaching those you have identified as important to your adoption process; who is important at a time that is important. So you might like to think about how you measure against the total number of potential adopters who might be engaged in the process and what you might mean by engagement (namely this doesn't necessarily mean they have made the change, just that they are involved). With regards timing, you may also like to consider how you use the niche strategy and then measure your progress in engaging others this way. Examples of engagement measures may include assessing the numbers attending meetings, conferences, training courses, involvement in audits, returns on questionnaires etc.

Process Measures help you check whether you are heading in the right direction. For example, if your aim is to improve chronic care, then one of the process measures might be to check how many practices have implemented registries. Many improvement projects use process measures as the mainstay of their work. You may decide to add in extra process measures for your spread phase and use these as a way of checking whether the spread process is being effective. For example, you may decide to measure a specific good practice and check the length of time it take for it to get adopted by a group. You might also measure the level of variation and customisation applied to a good idea as this will give you an idea of the extent of crossing the canyon and which type of group is adopting the practice.

Outcome measures are those that demonstrate impact. The whole reason why we're busting a gut and putting all this effort in is so we can make a difference – so what is it for? This measure needs to be clear and be the one that grabs the heart of those that are doing all the work. It needs to make sense to them and answer the question "Why?". When you've written it, see if you can add the phrase "so that" and complete the sentence. For example, "x% of patients to have an A1c below 7%, so that…", "reduce acute hospitalisations to 23%, so that…"

Step 4: Detail your plan. What this is depends on your goal, your constraints, resources and your measures. What it is likely not going to be is just a set of communication or information dissemination activities or only a few training events. Of course your plan of activities will change according to how you progress according to your measures.

A spread measurement plan at the high level is much like an improvement project plan in that you can treat it like PDSA cycles and test which strategies appear to work best to encourage engagement, which ones progress the process measures that lead to impact, and so on. Without a clear spread measurement plan you will be doing a lot of your work blind.

PREVENTING OCCURRENCES

Develop a measurement plan for spread that ties in directly with your intention, goals and aims. As spread is less precise than the detail of an improvement project I suggest you use the term *indicator* where you feel you are unable to use a precise number. Feel free to use ranges, and if you are uncertain about your numbers then put an uncertainty percentage next to the figure. It is much better to have a basic measurement plan than to have nothing at all. Without a plan I suggest you have no idea of the scope of what you intend to cover and thus no idea of when you will have achieved your target. Also this will help you focus on avoiding the low hanging fruit syndrome and many of the other issues we have covered in previous chapters.

Many of the "how" and theoretical models I see presented, and some of these include those I have previously taught, I feel have not expressly covered this pragmatic aspect of spread. This is a basic management, leadership and improvement aspect of managing large scale change programs.

PROGNOSIS

This is one area I get depressed about. I'm no numbers expert but I do know that what doesn't get measured usually doesn't get implemented. Somehow the measurement ethic has caught on in the quality improvement world, but when it comes to spread, which is now an add-on to QI, measurement seems to go out the window. The only measurement that sticks, if at all, is at the level of the project team. While this is useful, I believe it is insufficient. Spread is a high level concept and it needs some proper measurement to go with it if it is to be conceived and then applied. Either measurement is being skipped because it is not understood or because leaders feel it is not important or because it is felt to be too difficult. Whatever the reason, in my experience, the spread programs that have begun to use it are those that are beginning to demonstrate real discipline of application and impact.

FURTHER READING

I haven't found anything new published on spread measures but if you would like some thought-provoking and light reading about numbers then I can recommend... **Rimmer, G., How to Make a Camel Smoothie: And other Surreal Sums., Icon Books, 2005.**

Chapter 9

Lack of heart

PRESENTING SYMPTOMS

- Senior management don't seem to take an interest in the wider program or the project work that any of the teams are carrying out

- Once the flush of success of the original project has died down you're finding it difficult to keep anyone interested in the work underway, even though it is just as interesting and the results are possibly even better

- The project seems boring

DESCRIPTION

It had been a stimulating and active workshop with around a hundred primary care clinical leaders in the English National Health Service. As we were concluding, Paul, a General Practitioner took the microphone and said "So this means, to be an effective leader I probably need to step outside the norm and do things differently. It probably means taking risks and this means I won't be liked a lot of the time." His words were greeted with a very thoughtful silence and I so wanted to rush up and give him a hug. For I really believe he had in those words said something so ordinary, so straightforward, yet so incredibly important.

We had been working on how good ideas spread, communication techniques and the importance of personal influence. What Paul was intuitively keying into was the need for leaders to be one of a kind and of the personal pain that comes with that. Stepping up, maintaining one's values, speaking out, holding ground, all when under criticism and debate is a tough role.

What do I mean about the leader needing to be one of a kind? I wouldn't go quite as far as suggesting going for the Claude Cockburn theory of "Never believing anything until it is officially denied", however, there is something about the need to be your own person and not to be a copier.

Now that sounds like it goes against everything we think spread and adoption of good practice is about. But think of it like this. I believe the leader that enables the adoption of good practice is the one who can focus on the end result and who can differentiate the behaviours that enable the good practice, from the actual solution. Someone who can then customise like hell to make sure the solution is adapted to make it work **in their own context**. The leader who tries *to copy the solution* will have difficulty engaging their followers as well as implementing the change. So they need to be great customisers as well as great copiers; both/ands.

Maybe I've just seen too many spread programs and been to too many project reviews, too many collaborative workshops, and I don't know about you, but it seems countless teams are underwhelmed, uninspired, almost bored. Think about it. I don't mean overwhelmed by what they face, I mean underwhelmed by the potential of what they can achieve. Here we have in the room some of the most experienced and educated participants, who can each individually and jointly deliver a remarkable impact on the lives of others, yet it appears they are trapped in a limbo land, fearful of failure, and perhaps also fearing their success.

Maybe I'm being harsh, yet I am sure there is a nugget of truth that you recognise in this. The task of spreading good practice is to accelerate the benefits of good ideas so a wider patient group, and by consequence also healthcare staff, can feel the impact. Achieving this while lacking in motivation and inspiration is difficult, ranging to impossible.

So whose task is it to fix this problem? Bringing a "motivational" speaker along to the conference or workshop is a very temporary short term fix with unsustainable results. Ultimately the job in hand is for the members of the team, the organisation, for the individuals on the project team, for the leaders within, to find the appealing and remarkable thread that will provide the energising focus of attention, the grabber, the pull, the hook.

Without leadership spread programs founder very quickly. Who is the leader of a spread initiative? Firstly there is the high level program which someone is sponsoring. For some this may take the form of a large scale collaborative, for others is may look like the rollout of a single pilot program in a more traditional project format. There may be a steering group with a chair. Is there inspirational and leadership in this group sufficient to motivate not only the steering group but also the entire spread program, including all the constituent organisations and teams?

Secondly, each of the constituent organisations needs to have identified leadership, especially clinical leadership if the program has clinical content. By leadership I mean more than attendance at the odd meeting and signatures on expense statements and the corralling of participants to be involved on various projects. The intent is for a leader to demonstrate their passion for the topic under work, to be able to explain its importance, to justify its necessity and to do this with a personal interest and commitment.

Finally there will be other forms of leadership taking place within a spread program. As spread itself is so distributed, so will the leadership be – distributed. Many different leadership roles within teams may evolve and at different times. These are different to the project management roles which may be mostly administrative and co-ordinating.

SUGGESTED TREATMENT

Most spread programs that I have seen under development and in action tend to focus on a combination of improvement science skills and content knowledge. Occasionally some include leadership capabilities, though this an exception. Building this into programs is a necessity – at all levels, not just the organisation.

Where I do see leadership added into the curriculum it is often not specified what is meant as the leadership factors specific for a spread program. I have attempted to detail below some of the critical criteria that I believe are necessary. Of course, many other factors are also required.

Courage. Spreading good practice is no easy task. It is a scaling up task so something that is usually done on a large scale, even when it is implemented using small test cycles like PDSAs, the intent is for a large transformational change. So it needs big commitment when you start, knowing you intend to make big changes over a large scale. Never to be approached lightly, it is often more difficult than "new" change as there are many obstacles to taking on existing ideas.

What exactly do we mean by *courage* when referring to leadership? Perhaps it might be better to think of encouragement, to provide others with courage. *Courage* has its root in the latin word "cor" which means heart, so *encouragement*, means to provide others with heart. I think that having heart, *courage*, and providing others with heart, *encouragement*, is a good place for all spread leaders to start.

Curiosity. Inquisitive leaders continually seek out new ideas and ways round problems. They will find out how to customise a piece of good practice from elsewhere so that it works in their own situation. Curiosity also helps when you're trying to work out whether the problem you have is one of customising or copying. A leader like this will also be snooping about to see who is doing something better than they are. Curiosity is the opposite of apathy.

Passion. Think about a person who has inspired you in some way. When they talk about what it is that interests them something shines through. They sound almost but not quite obsessive about their topic. We know from research that if you want to influence someone 7-10% of the influence comes from the content about which you speak, 35-8% from your tone of voice and the rest, 65%, from your body language. The importance of letting your enthusiasm and zeal be portrayed is crucial if you are to take on the mantle of leadership at any level of your spread program.

Followership. Leaders must have followers to be effective; and in spread programs, the more followers, the more effective the spread, as in the greater the adoption in terms of number and speed, is likely to be. The relationship between the leader and the follower is symbiotic and communication needs to flow in both directions. It is no good for a leader to pronounce a vision and then leave it to a group to deliver. Discussions need to continue and there needs to be good feedback systems in place. Indeed, a lucky leader is one who has followers who will provide open and honest feedback.

Followers have responsibilities too – like giving feedback and accepting responsibilities and opportunities. The relationship between leader and follower is a delicate one and there is much written about it.

I am sure you will have many other competencies you will add to the above list. Those are the ones I feel are crucial. So how do we get these applied, in practice?

- Talk about these factors when you talk about leadership and what it means in terms of the spread of good practice.

- At the start of a spread phase seek out individuals who you feel have the factors listed above, who will be able to take the message forward.

- If you have a leadership role in spread work, then take heed of the importance of *courage, curiosity* and *passion*.

- What gets talked about tends to get done. Help organisational leaders develop their stories about the work in hand. In workshops, support them with developing their storytelling abilities. This may mean going as far as teaching them advanced storytelling techniques and helping them practice these. Also, help them by ensuring they are tapped into the information gathering process so they get early information on results from project.

- Inspiration and motivation is a face-to-face event, or at the very least it needs tone of voice, so a phone call is a minimum, and build in as much personal time and contact as is possible. Leaders at all levels need to have direct contact with the individuals and teams carrying out the work. The best activity for them in this contact is *praise* – catch the teams doing the right work.

PREVENTING OCCURRENCES

Teams that lose heart in their work are a loss to the organisation and to the healthcare community. The responsibility for lifting them up, carrying them forward and encouraging them lies squarely on the shoulders of leaders. Ensure you have these leaders patched into their roles and responsibilities at an early stage and that you are on the look out for emerging talent at all times.

PROGNOSIS

An inspirational team leader, an interested CEO, a passionate team member – I have seen them all be the one difference that has ensured their team or organisation has adopted changes when others haven't. When we've supplied complicated change packages, in depth workshops, lengthy support packages, it seems these individuals are the ones that can really make the difference.

The outlook? Get this right – get a whole lot right!

FURTHER READING

Annunzio, Susan Lucia, Contagious Success – Spreading High Performance Throughout your Organization, Penguin Books, 2004. What I liked about his book was the way it looked at the whole organisation and focused on high performing workgroups and elevated the importance of relationships and teams. This is where I believe the future lies. Excellent case studies from which to learn.

Chapter 10

Vision for the future

I thought long and hard about my personal vision for the future of how the spread of good practice would work. Realising that the last thing I wanted to do was contribute another theory or 'ology! In the end, I was influenced, like as at the start of this book, by a current events.

My local hospital hit the national press with a difficult Commission for Healthcare Improvement report following 41 deaths and 498 patients infected after three outbreaks of clostridium difficile. The press reports did not make for good reading.

At around the same time the Journal for Hospital Infection carried a report about how two researchers followed 71 staff on a hospital ward over a week, observing their hand washing habits. Although the staff knew they were being observed 22% were found not to wash their hands after contact with MRSA patients, 38% were found not to wash after contact with blood and 25% didn't wash after contact with patients' faeces.

There was little in the report about my local hospital that was not known knowledge or much in the Journal report that was not known good practice, yet for a variety of reasons it was not put into place. Some of these reasons are simple behavioural steps, i.e. habits, and others a little more complicated and down to organisational culture, namely a combination of even more behaviours and habits.

I named this book *Undressing the Elephant* because I believe there is an enormous elephant sitting in every meeting room, ward, clinic, hospital, primary care practice. This elephant is about *doing what we know we can do*. The nurses on the wards know how to wash their hands, they know what is best practice, but for some reason it doesn't get implemented. This is a large elephant and my intent in this book has been to undress it, to make it more visible so that its issues can be addressed. Dealing with the elephant will take some time; is taking time – far too much time.

In this final chapter I have set out my personal views regarding the "spread of good practice", as far as I have been able to construct them. I have put the phrase "spread of good practice" in quotes for a very specific reason. I wonder now whether I have been confusing the symptoms of the patient with the underlying cause. By this I mean, I wonder whether by continually thinking about how spread happens, or not, is focusing on a set of symptoms, when really it would be more helpful to look at what is actually happening in organisations – like the detail of what is going on to reduce HAI's. This sounds like the same thing though there is a difference. In one, the focus is on the methodology – the process, in the other, the attention is on implementation – the practice. The view is different, and this may matter.

I spent the first ten years of my working life in the oil industry. Twenty years ago the safety record there was far superior to that of healthcare today. Statistics show that hospitals are not good places to be in. We are not good at implementing the basics. For whatever reason, the existing models and methodologies we are using are insufficient in their efficiency of implementation. Some good work is underway. However, as is often the case with what are called "improvement initiatives" these are patch-worked across geography and not keeping pace with consumer demands.

My vision for the future is based on two dimensions, though before I can describe these I need to make a shift in language. In our new approach I feel it's useful to no longer talk of the "spread of good practice". Instead we are focused on **implementing better ideas**. This shift in language moves us away from the patriarchal push of ideas from one person to another. The use of the word *implementing* encourages an active process on behalf of both the potential adopters as well as those providing information. *Better ideas* moves away from the suggestion that there is a set of ideal practices which need no customisation or reinvention. As a phrase it also helps reduce the notion that what is being presented is one person's scheme to be implemented, bringing with it all the natural human resistance.

I've found it easy and acceptable to use language like "Organisational Implementation phase" or "Region-wide Implementation Phase" to describe what was previously called "spread phases". For many project participants this language has made sense to them and been clear and specific about the intent of phase.

I have been struck by two recurring patterns in healthcare projects and large scale programs in which I have been involved over the last ten years.

Firstly, the majority of the large scale programs set out to deal with basic issues. They are the most common problems facing organisations. This is to be expected as this is where the greatest return for investment will be found.

However, the second pattern I find is that left to their own devices and without sufficient data diagnostic work, the majority of improvement teams will start their work on the area of least impact, usually beginning somewhere where they will get a quick win or where they perceive they have a significant problem but where the overall payback is actually quite small. This was discussed in the second chapter of this book.

I am left with a rough view that over 80% of the topics for improvement are very common and are well known to most organisations. Yet when faced with the change process teams prefer to work on the exceptions within this 80% area. I believe this mismatch comes from a misunderstanding of the change process. There are two different dynamics at play here and if we can separate them, them we may be able to help teams work in different and more effective ways. Before, when all I thought about was spread, I couldn't see these dynamics. Now, when I think more about the implementation process, I can perceive something quite different. And this may be important for accelerating improvements within and across organisations.

In the first dimension we can think of taking the 80+% of what is known and **standardise** it in our organisations through known efficient and effective management implementation processes.

The second dimension challenges the linear, staging view of "spread" and replaces it with organisational and individual **learning** processes.

One of the dilemmas for an organisation is how to deliver its required improvements – through projects or regular team / departmental aims and objectives, the annual performance improvement process. In this book, I have already emphasised the management rollout perspective. I've wondered whether the domination of "improvement-by-project" may be holding back the investment in long term sustainable solutions. Some redesign projects appear to be workaround solutions which are then "spread" to others. For example, with the advent of technology, there may be systems able to take over some activities previously done by staff, or it may take longer to implement a change in roles but be worthwhile in the long term. Some changes may require solutions that cannot be implemented on a project basis because they require the whole organisation to change, namely they require a strategic change – in IT, human resources, union rules, building renovations, partnership contracts etc.

A predicament in healthcare, when it comes to the standardisation of tasks, is the level of professional autonomy. I believe it is time to cost this out. The dynamic which has teams wanting to work on exceptions, the 20%, when working on improvement projects, rather than working to fix the 80% is part of this problem. No one seems to want to work on what is perceived to be the more boring and basic issues. Yet it is these that take up most of the time in healthcare. It is these where we find most of our errors and problems. It is here where the majority of improvement programs appear, have their need, yet lack their current focus.

Highly reliable organisations such as those in the oil, air and nuclear industries learnt decades ago that to survive they needed to standardise and integrate as many procedures as possible so as to remove human error. This required a massive investment in time, cash and human resources. It means an organisation-led focus rather than a project by project initiative. In the late 1970s and 1980s when these industries made significant leaps in safety improvements they also went through major organisational and industry transformation. It was a strategic intent with industry led leadership. The industry knew, at times, that they would need to work together to find ways to solve their safety issues, else they would all fail.

Maybe part of the problem with safety issues in healthcare is they are relatively invisible. If there was a sign in Times Square in New York and Trafalgar Square in London, listing the names of all those dying of Hospital Acquired Infection – as they died – maybe that would attract the public, as well as hospital staff attention.

I have focused here on safety as it is one of the most basic issues to be resolved in healthcare. Until this one is satisfied, until "first do no harm" becomes the mantra, until safety really is first, then we are failing our patients and staff in the most basic of ways. All other improvement initiatives appear weak by comparison.

My vision for this first dimension is as organisations we identify the significant potential for improvement through standardisation and that we implement this through organisational strategies rather than through smaller project based initiatives. Much of what we need to know is already out there ready to be found. The knowledge is available. How can we develop a cadre of seekers who are goal driven, to go and find out what we need to know, when we need it? Then take this knowledge and build it into the existing structures of the organisation, ensuring that policies, procedures and all performance requirements have this built in as a requirement. This won't be enough as there needs to be learning systems enabled and this leads me to the next aspect.

This second dimension relates more to how individuals and teams take the knowledge and use it. With hindsight I see two "industries" at work. One has been producing knowledge, like clinical guidelines or designing what might be regarded as "good practice" and then another which is designed as a process to enable change capability – to put the knowledge into practice. The success of delivering improvement has been the balance between these. Too much knowledge and not enough change capability in the organisation and the local reaction has been something akin to a catatonic response. Individuals and teams get overwhelmed so they do nothing with the information. On the other hand, those who are enthusiastically subsumed by the process of change and may even have too little information or good ideas about what to do tend to be quite uncoordinated about their approach and can cause a great deal of anxiety and change fatigue in a system. Getting this balance right is an important part in any implementation phase and is one which needs an effective organisational leadership.

A traditional view of spread I frequently encounter has this linear view that one carries out a project, gets some results and then moves onto a spread phase when the results are then "spread" on to others.

Without a doubt there are many large programs that are achieving results using this method. My issue is whether this is enough in terms of breadth and speed. These programs tend to work on one issue, one topic area and take twelve to eighteen months to deliver results. We need to find more efficient and effective ways to deliver results. Both within organisations and in the industry.

In the first dimension I saw 80+% of the improvement needs being delivered through standardisation of work tasks. The rest I see here, being delivered through the enabling of learning individuals and learning teams. Here we are attending to basic behavioural skills. In the case of the hand washing example at the beginning of this chapter, one way to improve performance would be to provide feedback to the nurses so they can increase their awareness of their behaviour. There are many ways that feedback can be added to their system to help them learn new behaviours so they can have improved consequences. They can provide feedback to one another. They can pair up, asking each other for feedback, developing curiosity about their hand washing behaviour, knowing how important it is. They can be video'd and then be encouraged to review their own videos and see their own behaviour. They can list the names of their own patients who have developed a HAI and keep a reflective diary. I am sure there are other methods where they personally raise their own awareness and develop their own methods of feedback. I don't believe that more training will help them, or their patients, in the longer term.

This system of providing feedback to increase awareness can be used in all areas where standardisation is not directly applicable, where there are no identified better ideas, or where awareness needs to be improved as to what the standard practice needs to be.

Keeping with the behavioural model, if new better ideas are proposed, then one of the fast ways to help them get adopted is to identify what behaviours need to be changed as part of the adopted process. This is not quite as straightforward as it sounds and is an excellent analytical task to perform. For example, if a new clinical guideline is proposed then rather than just sending it out for implementation, a useful step is for a small group to get together and work through it asking the question for each step in the guideline, *"For this to be adopted, to be implemented well, whose behaviour has to change and how does it have to change?"* By making a list of the behaviours and who exactly is involved this type of action plan will give an idea of the extent of activity required to implement this guideline. It will also focus it at the level of people and behaviours, rather than tasks and activities. In my experience this has helped the adoption process, especially when this information is drafted by the group that develops the initial ideas. This information can then be revised by the adopting group to customise it.

As an individual we can also focus on our decision making process. How we go about deciding what to adopt, why and when to do so is an interesting process. If we can personally increase our reflective acts and learn to share these we can increase the learning capital of the team we are in.

If our teams are not co-located then it is helpful to think about them as virtual teams and then to consider what technological support they might need. This links closely to the chapter on the nini's. My experience in healthcare suggests there is a dearth of support for virtual teams. The facility to make conference calls, video conferencing and a variety of internet tools. One exception I know of is the Department of Veteran Affairs in the USA which has some impressive virtual training and meeting facilities. Let's remember that technology changes with the times and that staff will need training on how to make the best use of it.

In summary, to implement better ideas, I'd like to see organisational leaders show the way by integrating standardisation into the day-to-day work of the organisation. They'll demonstrate courage, curiosity and passion as they substantially reinvent and reengineer solutions to ensure they fit in their local context, thus enabling wide adoption and improved performance. Leaders at all levels will collaborate with their industry counterparts to create the movement necessary to reshape what is currently not fit for purpose so they no longer carry out marginal improvements.

I'd anticipate teams working both face-to-face and virtually in new ways that mean they challenge their existing practices, seek out better ideas and emphasise compassionate care. I'd like to see teams proactively seeking existing better ideas to solve their problems, guided by current technology and their own curiosity and caring principles; and for these actions to be within an organisational performance framework. I'd expect individuals to accept responsibility for the consequences of their behaviour by raising their awareness through constantly eliciting feedback, including measuring clinical and administrative performance.

I expect implementing better ideas to be everybody's business.

Many people were involved in this book. Basically everyone I've worked with for the last two to three years has contributed in some way, through helping my thinking develop. Others read through the script and made some very helpful comments. I would like to thank you all.

The opinions in the book are all my own.

I am ever indebted to my husband, Ian, who as always reads the scripts, proofreads them, and patiently puts up with late meal times as my writing distracts me.